KU-518-022

M·E·N·U · M·A·S·T·E·R·S

VEGETARIAN MEALS

EDITED BY
ANNA JAMES

OCTOPUS BOOKS

MENU-MATCH CODE

To allow more flexibility within the menus we have added bold numbers after certain recipes to offer suitable alternatives.

Thus, if the numbers ·3·11·14· appear after a starter, they indicate that the starter of Menu 3, 11, or 14 could be substituted.

Using the MENU-MATCH CODE you will be sure to find a menu to suit all tastes.

NOTES

Standard spoon measurements are used in all recipes
1 tablespoon – one 15 ml spoon
1 teaspoon – one 5 ml spoon
All spoon measures are level

Where amounts of salt and pepper are not specified, the cook should use her own discretion.

Canned foods should not be drained, unless so stated in the recipe. For all recipes, quantities are given in metric and imperial measures. Follow one set of measures only, because they are not interchangeable.

A vegetarian Cheddar-type cheese may be substituted for any of the cheeses used in the recipes.

Wholemeal flour may be used throughout unless otherwise stated.

Jacket photograph: Hungarian spinach pancakes; Wholewheat salad; Mixed melon salad; Paprika soup.

First published 1986 by
Octopus Books Limited
59 Grosvenor Street, London W1

ISBN 0 7064 2659 2

Produced by Mandarin Publishers Ltd
22a Westlands Rd
Quarry Bay, Hong Kong
Printed in Hong Kong

C · O · N · T · E · N · T · S

I·N·T·R·O·D·U·C·T·I·O·N

The number of vegetarians in the Western world is on the increase and even if you are not a convinced vegetarian yourself, the chances are that you number several among your family or friends.

In the past vegetarians in 'mixed' company often got, quite literally, a raw deal – a salad or cheese platter. Eating out, for many vegetarians, was a lot less exciting than eating in, unless their hosts happened to be vegetarians too.

Today's cooks are more considerate and are far more likely to tailor an entire meal to the lone vegetarian, enjoying the challenge of producing dishes so delicious that everyone will enjoy them.

One of the major considerations for following a partial if not total vegetarian diet is health. A vegetarian diet is low in fats and high in fibre; it also tends to include more natural foods, more raw foods and fewer calories than the average diet followed by those who patronise the butcher more than the greengrocer.

In this book we've compiled 15 marvellous menus for all occasions. Each menu has a countdown, which tells you what to prepare when. In most cases the workload is spread over several days to make the meals as simple as possible to produce. Many of the dishes can be cooked ahead and frozen – consult the freezer notes for details.

Have fun!

M·E·N·U

·1·

Easy Summer Supper for 6

Vegetable Lasagne
Caesar Salad
Apple and Celeriac Salad
•
Peach Gâteau

On long lazy summer evenings it is great to entertain but no hostess wants to be held captive in the kitchen while her guests sip punch on the patio. The answer lies in planning ahead and combining fresh and frozen dishes so cleverly that guests will marvel at how you manage to produce so superb a spread without appearing to spend any time at all in the kitchen.

Choosing Wisely

Try to choose at least two courses which can be made ahead and frozen. The Vegetable Lasagne that is the star of this menu freezes so successfully that it will fool many a guest into thinking it has been freshly made. It consists of layers of pasta with a tasty mixture of vegetables, herbs, tomatoes and wine, topped with a cheese sauce. Serve it simply with wholewheat French bread and butter or hot garlic bread and salads.

Sweet Surrender

It is a popular myth that vegetarians end every meal with fresh fruit and self denial but it simply isn't true. Most vegetarians love a luscious dessert and few will be able to resist Peach Gâteau. The base can be made in advance and frozen until required. A sangria or fruit punch would be perfect for this meal. Alternatively, serve a crisp white wine such as Vinho Verde or Soave.

Vegetable Lasagne

Metric/Imperial

4 tablespoons olive oil
3 large onions, sliced
2 cloves garlic, peeled and crushed
500 g/1 lb tomatoes, skinned, seeded and chopped
150 ml/¼ pint dry white wine
2 teaspoons chopped fresh basil
2 teaspoons chopped fresh parsley
2 teaspoons chopped fresh marjoram
salt
freshly ground black pepper
1 tablespoon tomato paste
350 g/12 oz courgettes, sliced
250 g/8 oz shelled broad beans
125 g/4 oz shelled fresh peas

Sauce:
600 ml/1 pint milk
2 carrots, roughly chopped
1 leek, roughly chopped
1 small onion, roughly chopped
1 bay leaf
few peppercorns
50 g/2 oz butter or margarine
50 g/2 oz plain flour
2 teaspoons French mustard
175 g/6 oz Cheddar cheese, grated
50 g/2 oz Gruyère cheese, grated
1 tablespoon grated Parmesan cheese
500 g/1 lb spinach or egg lasagne
flat-leafed parsley, to serve

Vegetable lasagne

1. Heat half the oil in a pan, add the onions and garlic and fry gently for 7 to 8 minutes until lightly browned. Add the tomatoes and wine, bring to the boil, then simmer, uncovered, for 20 minutes. Add the herbs and salt and pepper to taste. Cook for a further 5 minutes, then stir in the tomato paste, courgettes, broad beans and peas and cook for a further 5 minutes. Remove from the heat and leave to cool.
2. Put the milk, carrots, leek, onion, bay leaf, salt and peppercorns in a pan. Bring to the boil, then remove from the heat and leave to infuse until cold. Strain the milk and reserve.
3. Melt the butter or margarine in a clean pan, add the flour and cook for 2 minutes, stirring all the time. Remove from the heat and gradually add the infused milk, beating vigorously after each addition. Return to the heat and bring to the boil, stirring constantly. Lower the heat, add the mustard and cheeses and simmer, stirring, until the cheese has melted. Taste and adjust seasoning.
4. Cook the lasagne in batches in boiling salted water with the remaining olive oil for 10 minutes. Drain and cool under cold running water, then drain well again.
5. Arrange a layer of pasta in the base of a lightly greased ovenproof dish. Spoon over some of the vegetable mixture, then top with another layer of pasta and cover with a layer of cheese sauce. Continue with these layers until all the ingredients are used up, finishing with cheese sauce.
6. Cook in a preheated oven (200°C/400°F), Gas Mark 6, for 40 minutes until bubbling and golden. Serve immediately, garnished with parsley. ·3·10·13·

Cook's Tip:
Look out for the 'no-cook' lasagne now available in supermarkets. Omit stage 4 and simply layer the raw pasta with the sauce mixture.

If fresh herbs are unavailable, add finely chopped watercress, spring onions or fresh coriander.

Caesar Salad

Metric/Imperial
120 ml/4 fl oz French dressing (page 55)
1 clove garlic, peeled
2 tablespoons oil
3 slices of bread, cut into small dice
2 cos lettuces, separated into leaves
50 g/2 oz Parmesan cheese, grated

1. In a screw-topped jar, combine the French dressing and garlic. Leave for at least 1 hour.
2. Heat the oil in a frying pan. Add the diced bread and fry for 3 to 4 minutes, turning constantly, or until the croûtons are crisp and lightly browned. Remove from the heat. Drain the croûtons on absorbent kitchen paper and allow to cool.
3. Tear the lettuce leaves into small pieces and place in a salad bowl. Remove and discard the garlic from the dressing and pour the dressing over the lettuce leaves. Toss to coat well. Sprinkle over the cheese and top with the croûtons. Serve at once. ·9·13·15·

Apple and Celeriac Salad

Metric/Imperial
750 g/1½ lb celeriac
1 teaspoon salt
5 tablespoons mayonnaise
1 tablespoon finely chopped fresh parsley
2 crisp red eating apples, cored and thinly sliced
125 g/4 oz salted cashew nuts, finely chopped
25 g/1 oz flaked almonds, toasted

1. Put the celeriac in a saucepan and cover with water. Add the salt. Bring to the boil, reduce the heat and cook for 15 minutes. Drain thoroughly, allow to cool, then slice thinly.
2. Mix together the mayonnaise and parsley. Add the apple, nuts and celeriac slices and stir to coat. Transfer to a salad bowl and serve. ·2·4·15·

Peach Gâteau

Metric/Imperial
3 eggs, separated
125 g/4 oz caster sugar
finely grated rind and juice of 1/2 lemon
50 g/2 oz semolina
25 g/1 oz ground almonds
To Serve:
4 ripe peaches, stoned and thinly sliced
300 ml/1/2 pint double cream, whipped
4 tablespoons apricot jam
2 teaspoons lemon juice
50 g/2 oz ground hazelnuts, toasted

1. Grease a deep 20 cm/8 inch cake tin, line the base with greaseproof paper, then grease the paper. Dust the inside of the tin lightly with flour.
2. Put the egg yolks, sugar, lemon rind and juice in a bowl and whisk until thick and mousse-like. Stir in the semolina and ground almonds. Whisk the egg whites until stiff, then fold in.
3. Turn the mixture into the prepared tin and level the surface. Bake in a preheated oven (180°C/350°F), Gas Mark 4, for 35 to 40 minutes until the cake springs back when lightly pressed in the centre. Turn out onto a wire rack, peel off the lining paper, turn the cake the right way up and leave to cool.
4. Cut the cake into 2 layers. Fold half of the peach slices into three quarters of the cream and use to sandwich the layers together.
5. Put the apricot jam and lemon juice in a small pan and heat gently, stirring, until the jam has melted. Sieve and reheat. Arrange the remaining peach slices on top of the cake. Brush the peaches and the sides of the cake with the warm glaze. Press the hazelnuts around the sides, then pipe the remaining cream around the top. Serve chilled. ·9·13·

Variation:
This gâteau is best made with fresh peaches, but when out of season, canned fruit may be used.

C · O · U · N · T · D · O · W · N

The day before:
Make the lasagne. When cool, cover with cling film and refrigerate. Make the dressing for the Caesar Salad – store at room temperature. Fry the croûtons, drain well and cool. Keep in an airtight container, bake the cake base for the Peach Gâteau and store in an airtight tin.

On the day:
Prepare the greens for the Caesar Salad and store in polythene bags in the refrigerator. Make the Apple and Celeriac Salad, cover and refrigerate. Prepare the punch, if serving.

To serve at 8.00 pm:
6.00: Assemble and decorate the Peach Gâteau and place in the refrigerator.
7.00: Preheat the oven to (200°C/400°F), Gas Mark 6. Chill the white wine.
7.20: Place the lasagne in the oven.
7.50: Remove the garlic from the dressing and toss the Caesar Salad. Finish with the cheese and croûtons.
8.00: Take the wines or punch to the table. Garnish the lasagne and serve with the salads and chunks of wholewheat French bread.

F · R · E · E · Z · E · R · N · O · T · E · S

Vegetable Lasagne: Make to the end of stage 5. Cool, then open freeze. Pack in a polythene bag, seal, label and freeze. When required, thaw at room temperature for 5-6 hours. Cook as directed.
Cake base for Gâteau: Open freeze, then wrap in cling film and overwrap in a plastic bag. Seal, label and return to the freezer for up to 4 months. Thaw in wrappings for 3-4 hours at room temperature.

Cook's Tip:
Try this refreshing summer punch. Peel and segment 3 oranges and place the segments in a large jug with a few ice cubes. Pour over 1 standard bottle chilled dry white wine, 500 ml/17 fl oz sparkling mineral water and 5 tablespoons Grand Marnier. Serve.

M·E·N·U

· 2 ·

Mediterranean Meal for 6

Spinach Triangles

•

Baked Fennel with Olives
Beetroot Salad
Cucumber Salad

•

Frosted Almond Creams

Every nation has its fund of vegetarian recipes, but the Mediterranean is a particularly rich source. The peoples of this region realised long ago that you don't need meat to make a meal memorable and they have evolved some marvellous dishes based upon simple ingredients such as cheese, yogurt, pasta and grains combined with sun-ripened vegetables, herbs and wines.

Filo Pastry

This menu begins with a Greek speciality – Spinach Triangles. A rich creamy spinach and cheese filling is enclosed in filo, a fine strudel-type pastry which is available in sheets from most good delicatessens. Filo dries out very quickly, so work with only one or two sheets at a time and keep the rest covered in cling film or wrapped in damp tea-towels. Puff pastry can be used if filo is not available but it must be rolled paper thin.

Setting the Scene

Cork place mats and colourful earthenware pottery would create a suitable simple setting for this Mediterranean meal.

Spinach Triangles

Metric/Imperial
250 g/8 oz filo pastry
50 g/2 oz butter or margarine, melted
Filling:
500 g/1 lb fresh spinach
15 g/½ oz butter or margarine
50 g/2 oz curd cheese
25 g/1 oz Gruyère cheese, grated
1 tablespoon grated Parmesan cheese
2 tablespoons double cream
1 egg
1 egg yolk
pinch of freshly grated nutmeg
salt
freshly ground black pepper
To Serve:
a little melted butter
coriander leaves

1. Cook the spinach in a covered saucepan, with just the water clinging to the leaves after washing, for 6 to 8 minutes until tender. Drain, and squeeze dry, then chop the spinach finely. Melt the 15 g/½ oz butter or margarine in a pan, stir in the spinach and heat through gently. Remove from the heat and beat in the cheeses, cream, eggs, nutmeg, and season.
2. Cut one sheet of filo pastry lengthways into 7.5 cm/3 inch wide strips. Brush one strip with melted butter, put a rounded teaspoon of filling about 2.5 cm/1 inch in from one end, then fold the corner over the filling to make a triangle. Fold the remaining strip over and over to make a little fat triangular package. Continue this process with the remaining pastry, melted butter and filling.
3. Place the triangles on a baking sheet. Brush with the remaining melted butter or margarine and bake in a preheated oven (200°C/400°F), Gas Mark 6, for 15 to 20 minutes until golden brown. Garnish with coriander leaves and serve immediately. ·8·15·

Baked Fennel with Olives

Metric/Imperial
4 medium fennel bulbs, trimmed
2 tablespoons oil
2 medium onions, finely chopped
2 cloves garlic, peeled and crushed
350 g/12 oz tomatoes, skinned, seeded and chopped
¼ teaspoon chopped fresh thyme
1 bay leaf
150 ml/¼ pint vegetable stock
salt
freshly ground black pepper
50 g/2 oz black olives, stoned
75 g/3 oz Gruyère cheese, grated

1. Place the fennel bulbs in a pan of boiling, salted water and cook for about 20 minutes. Drain, refresh under cold running water and drain well again. Cut each bulb in halves or quarters.
2. Heat the oil in a pan, add the onions and garlic and cook until soft but not coloured. Add the tomatoes, thyme, bay leaf, stock, salt and pepper. Cover and cook over a gentle heat for 10 to 15 minutes. Discard the bay leaf.
3. Place the fennel and olives in a casserole. Coat with the sauce. Cover, place in a preheated oven (180°C/350°F), Gas Mark 4 and cook for 30 minutes or until the fennel is quite tender.
4. Sprinkle the cheese over the top. Increase the oven temperature to 200°C/400°F, Gas Mark 6, and cook, uncovered, for a further 15 minutes until the cheese has melted and browned. Alternatively, place under a preheated grill and brown.

Variation:
If fennel is unobtainable or out of season use 1 large head of celery. Wash and roughly chop the celery. Cook the celery according to stage 1 for 10 minutes only. Continue as for fennel.

Spinach triangles

Beetroot Salad

Metric/Imperial
¼ small red cabbage, shredded
125 g/4 oz pickled beetroot, cut into strips
50 g/2 oz French beans, cooked
1 tablespoon chopped fresh marjoram
Dressing:
3 tablespoons olive oil
1 tablespoon wine vinegar
1 teaspoon coriander seeds, crushed
salt

1. Mix together the red cabbage, beetroot, French beans and marjoram in a salad bowl.
2. In a screw-top jar, mix the oil, vinegar, coriander seeds and salt. Shake well. Pour over the vegetables and toss well. ·4·9·13·

Cucumber Salad

Metric/Imperial
1 cucumber, peeled and very thinly sliced
2 teaspoons salt
1 clove garlic, peeled and crushed
1 tablespoon wine vinegar
120 ml/4 fl oz plain yogurt
1 tablespoon vegetable oil
1 tablespoon chopped fresh dill

1. Put the cucumber in a colander. Sprinkle it with half of the salt and allow it to drain for 1 hour.
2. Blend together the garlic and vinegar. Add the remaining salt and mix to a smooth paste. Stir in the yogurt, oil and dill.
3. Pour this yogurt dressing over the well-drained cucumber. Toss well and chill before serving. ·14·

Frosted Almond Creams

Metric/Imperial
2 eggs, separated
50 g/2 oz soft brown sugar
50 g/2 oz chopped almonds, toasted
300 ml/½ pint plain yogurt
2 tablespoons Grand Marnier
To Decorate:
25 g/1 oz toasted slivered almonds

1. Beat the egg yolks and soft brown sugar together until thick and creamy. Stir in the chopped almonds, plain yogurt and liqueur. Beat the egg whites until just stiff, then fold into the almond mixture. Pour into 6 individual freezerproof dishes and freeze until firm about 2 to 3 hours.
2. To serve: remove from the freezer and leave to soften slightly at room temperature for 15 minutes, or in the refrigerator for approximately 30 minutes. Sprinkle with the toasted slivered almonds before serving. ·10·

Variation:
Try an almond-flavoured liqueur such as Amaretto de Saronno to replace the Grand Marnier in Frosted Almond Creams.
For a simpler accompaniment, serve slices of fresh pineapple, watermelon or mango.

C · O · U · N · T · D · O · W · N

The day before:
Make the filling for the Spinach Triangles. Cool, cover and refrigerate. Make the dressing for the Beetroot Salad – store at room temperature. Prepare the yogurt dressing for the Cucumber Salad, cover and refrigerate. Make the Frosted Almond Creams and freeze until firm. Toast the almonds for the topping and store in an airtight container.
On the day:
Complete the Spinach Triangles. Place them on a baking sheet and brush with melted butter. Keep in the refrigerator until required. Prepare the fennel and the sauce and combine them with the olives in a casserole. Cover and refrigerate. Prepare all the vegetables for the Beetroot Salad and store separately, covered, in the refrigerator. Chop the fresh herbs and set aside at room temperature. Salt and drain the cucumber for the Cucumber Salad, then cover with cling film and place in the refrigerator until needed.
To serve at 8.00 pm:
6.00: Open the wines. If you have pre-cooked and frozen the Spinach Triangles, transfer them to the refrigerator to thaw.
7.00: Preheat the oven to (180°C/350°F), Gas Mark 4. Complete the Cucumber Salad, toss gently and return to the refrigerator.
7.15: Cover the fennel dish with foil and place it in the oven. Combine the vegetables for the Beetroot Salad, add the dressing and toss well. Cover and refrigerate.
7.40: Raise the oven temperature to 200°C/400°F, Gas Mark 6.
7.45: Add the topping to the fennel dish and return it to the oven with the Spinach Triangles. Transfer the Frosted Almond Creams from the freezer to the refrigerator to soften.
7.55: Decorate the almond creams with the almonds and return them to the refrigerator. Place the wines on the table.
8.00: Remove the fennel dish from the oven and keep warm. Transfer the Spinach Triangles to a warm serving platter and serve the meal.

F · R · E · E · Z · E · R · N · O · T · E · S

Spinach Triangles: Open freeze, then pack in rigid containers, seal and label. Store for up to 3 months. Can be cooked from frozen (allow 35-40 minutes at 200°C/400°F, Gas Mark 6) or thaw for about 1½ hours in the refrigerator before proceeding as in the recipe.
Frosted Almond Creams: Cover, seal and freeze for up to 3 months. Allow to soften before serving.

M·E·N·U

· 3 ·

After-work Supper for 6

Herb Gnocchi with Peperonata
Artichoke Salad
Fennel Salad
Quick Wholemeal Bread
•
Lemon Lattice Flan

There are cooks and there are conjurors – people who invite you to drop in for a bite after work, arrive as you do, and then proceed to produce an excellent meal in less time and with apparently less effort than it takes you to down an aperitif.

This menu could make you that kind of reputation. It features Herb Gnocchi, served with a delicious pepper sauce and accompanied by two unusual salads and a home-made wholewheat loaf. Everything appears to be freshly cooked – the mystery to your guests will be how you managed without magic. The secret is, of course, planning and preparation, all of which is clearly detailed in the countdown that follows.

Late Option

We've elected to serve the meal at 8 pm but the menu would be equally suitable for a late night supper, after a trip to the theatre, perhaps. The gnocchi is light and easily digested. Serve it as suggested here or simply, with melted butter and grated Parmesan cheese. If time is really at a premium, abandon the idea of making your own bread. Brush a bakery loaf lightly with water, wrap it in foil and heat it in a warm oven for 10-15 minutes. Accompany the meal with an Italian full-bodied red wine, such as Lambrusco or Barolo.

Herb Gnocchi

Metric/Imperial
250 g/8 oz spinach
125 g/4 oz sorrel
1 bunch watercress
50 g/2 oz fresh parsley
1 tablespoon chopped fresh tarragon
175 g/6 oz ricotta cheese
25 g/1 oz butter or margarine, diced
75 g/3 oz Parmesan cheese, grated
salt
freshly ground black pepper
2 eggs, beaten
3 tablespoons plain wholemeal flour, sifted
melted butter, to serve

1. Wash and drain the spinach, sorrel, watercress and parsley. Place in a large pan of boiling water and boil for 4 minutes; drain. When cool enough to handle, press out as much moisture as possible and chop finely. Add the tarragon and place in a saucepan over a low heat for several minutes, stirring, to dry out.
2. Beat the ricotta cheese to a smooth consistency and add to the purée with the butter or margarine, 25 g/1 oz of the Parmesan cheese and salt and pepper to taste. Take the pan off the heat and stir in the eggs and flour. Beat until smooth. Pour into a cool shallow dish and leave in the refrigerator overnight.
3. Bring a large pan of lightly salted water to the boil. Form the green mixture into egg-shaped gnocchi, using 2 teaspoons, and roll them very lightly on a floured board. Drop them in batches in the pan, but do not crowd them.
4. When they float to the surface, after 4 to 5 minutes, lift them out with a slotted spoon and drain on a cloth.
5. Sprinkle the gnocchi with a little of the Parmesan cheese. Serve with melted butter and Peperonata. ·1·9·

Peperonata

Metric/Imperial
150 ml/¼ pint olive oil
1 kg/2 lb red and green peppers, cored, seeded and sliced
1 large onion, sliced
500 g/1 lb tomatoes, skinned and sliced
2 cloves garlic, peeled and chopped
salt
freshly ground black pepper

1. Heat the oil in a large pan, add the vegetables and garlic, cover and cook gently for 15 minutes. Add salt and pepper to taste, and cook for a further 10 minutes. Serve hot with the gnocchi. ·8·10·

Cook's Tip:
Pepéronata is a useful dish because it can be made in advance and reheated, it is also excellent as a filling for pancakes. For a light lunch or supper, serve it hot or cold with crusty brown bread and a green salad.

Artichoke Salad

Metric/Imperial
1 crisp lettuce
2 sticks celery, sliced
75 g/3 oz stuffed olives
1 × 397 g/14 oz can artichoke hearts, drained
Dressing:
2 tablespoons olive oil
1 tablespoon lemon juice
salt
freshly ground black pepper

1. Wash the lettuce, drain and pat dry. Break into pieces and place in a bowl with the celery and olives.
2. Cut the artichoke hearts in half lengthwise and add to the lettuce.
3. In a screw-top jar, mix the oil, lemon juice, salt and pepper. Shake well. Just before serving, toss the salad with the dressing. ·1·4·15·

Fennel Salad

Metric/Imperial
175 g to 250 g/6 to 8 oz courgettes, sliced
salt
2 large fennel, thinly sliced
250 g/8 oz French beans, sliced and cooked
6 stuffed green olives
Dressing:
150 ml/¼ pint soured cream
1 teaspoon whole-grain mustard

1. Put the courgette slices on a plate, sprinkle with salt and leave for 15 minutes to draw out the excess moisture. Rinse and thoroughly dry the courgette slices and place them in the bottom of a salad bowl. Place the fennel on top, then the beans.
2. Mix the soured cream with the mustard and pour it over the salad. Chill before serving. ·2·9·13·

Quick Wholemeal Bread

Metric/Imperial
250 g/8 oz plain flour
2 teaspoons salt
1 teaspoon bicarbonate of soda
350 g/12 oz wholemeal flour
300 ml/½ pint buttermilk
4 tablespoons water

1. Sift the plain flour, salt and soda into a bowl. Mix in the wholemeal flour, then add the buttermilk and water. Mix to a soft dough.
2. Turn the dough onto a floured surface, knead lightly until smooth, then shape into a large round, 4 cm/1½ inches thick. Place on a floured baking sheet and sprinkle with flour.
3. Bake in a preheated oven (220°C/425°F), Gas Mark 7, for 25 minutes. Cool on a wire rack. ·4·

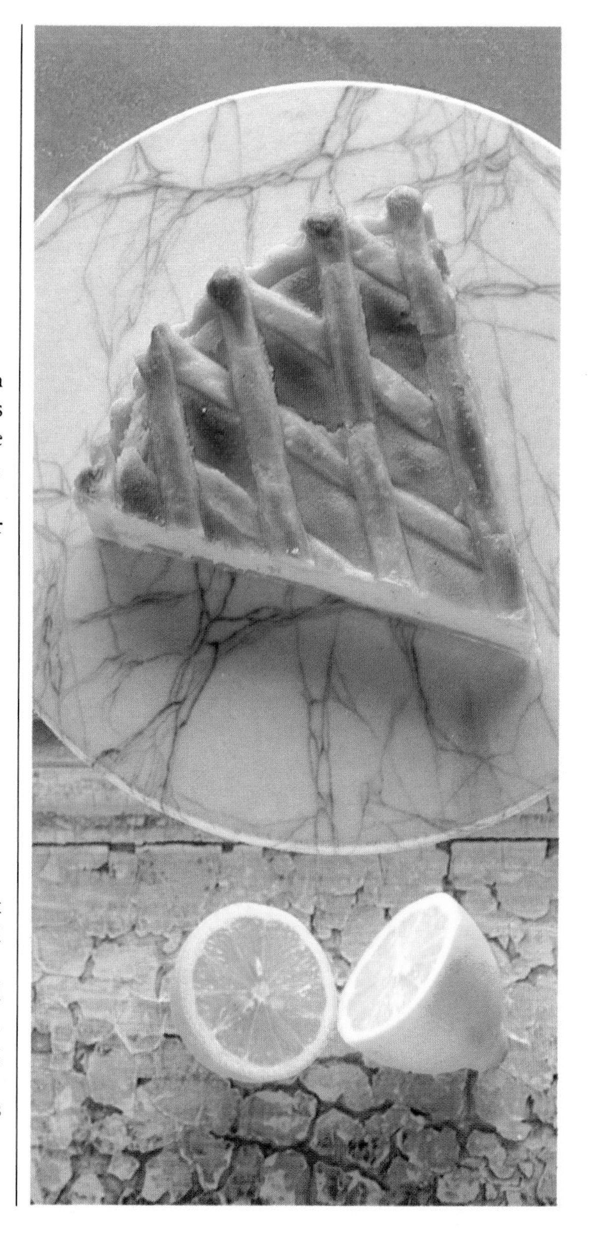

Lemon lattice flan

Lemon Lattice Flan

Metric/Imperial
250 g/8 oz plain flour
150 g/5 oz butter or margarine
1 tablespoon caster sugar
1 egg yolk
1 to 2 tablespoons iced water
Filling:
125 g/4 oz butter or margarine
125 g/4 oz caster sugar
finely grated rind and juice of 2 lemons
4 egg yolks
125 g/4 oz ground almonds
120 ml/4 fl oz double cream

1. Sift the flour into a bowl. Rub in the butter or margarine until the mixture resembles fine breadcrumbs. Stir in the sugar. Add the egg yolk and enough water to mix to a fairly stiff dough.
2. Turn the dough onto a floured surface and knead lightly until smooth. Roll out and use to line a 20 cm/8 inch fluted flan ring placed on a baking sheet. Reserve the trimmings. Chill the flan and trimmings in the refrigerator for 30 minutes.
3. Prick the base of the dough and line with foil and baking beans. Bake 'blind' in a preheated oven (200°C/400°F), Gas Mark 6, for 15 minutes, then remove the foil and beans and return the flan to the oven for a further 5 minutes. Leave to cool. Lower the oven temperature to 180°C/350°F, Gas Mark 4.
4. Cream the butter or margarine, sugar and lemon rind together until light and fluffy. Beat in the egg yolks, almonds, lemon juice and cream. Turn into the pastry case and level the surface.
5. Roll out the reserved pastry trimmings and cut into narrow strips. Use these to make a lattice pattern over the filling.
6. Brush with egg glaze. Bake for 20 to 25 minutes until golden brown. Leave to cool slightly, then remove from the flan ring. Serve warm. ·4·

C · O · U · N · T · D · O · W · N

The day before:
Prepare the gnocchi to the end of stage 2. Cool, cover and refrigerate overnight. Make the Peperonata, cool, cover and store in the refrigerator. Bake the flan case and when cool, set aside at room temperature.
On the day:
Combine all the ingredients for the Artichoke Salad, except the dressing, in a salad bowl. Cover and refrigerate. Salt the courgettes for the Fennel Salad, rinse and dry them and arrange in a salad bowl with the fennel and beans. Cover and refrigerate. Make the Quick Wholemeal Bread, leave to cool on a wire rack. Make the flan filling, cover and keep in the refrigerator.
To serve at 8.00 pm:
6.45: Preheat the oven to (180°C/350°F), Gas Mark 4. Fill the flan and brush the lattice with egg. Open the red wines.
7.00: Place the flan in the oven to bake, or, if cooking the flan from frozen, turn the oven temperature down to 180°C/350°F, Gas Mark 4.
7.20: If cooked, remove the flan from the ring, place on a serving plate and keep warm. Reduce the oven temperature to 150°C/300°F, Gas Mark 2.
7.30: Reheat the Peperonata gently in a saucepan. Shape and cook the gnocchi. Keep warm in the oven.
7.55: Add the dressings to the salads and toss them.
8.00: Serve the meal.

F · R · E · E · Z · E · R · N · O · T · E · S

Quick Wholemeal Bread: Prepare the dough to the end of stage 2. Wrap the bread in cling film, seal, label and freeze. Thaw overnight at cool room temperature and bake as in stage 3.
Lemon Lattice Flan: Open freeze uncooked, when frozen. Wrap. To use, bake from frozen in a preheated oven (200°C/400°F), Gas Mark 6 for 15 minutes. Reduce the oven temperature to 180°C/350°F, Gas Mark 4 and bake for a further 20-25 minutes until golden brown. Cool and remove from the flan ring.

M·E·N·U

· 4 ·

Home-coming Meal for 6

Thick Bean Soup
Tomato Salad
Endive Salad
Cheese and Chive Bread
•
Pear Tart Frangipane

When you've spent a day in the country, or an afternoon walking on a windswept beach, there's nothing to beat a warming bowl of soup with a wedge of home-made bread. Add a couple of fresh salads and a delectable dessert and you have a meal whose memory will linger long after all the anoraks have dried and the last blister has healed.

Cheap and Cheerful

This menu is good news for the cook. Despite its lavish appearance, the thick bean soup costs little, is easy to make and freezes exceptionally well. So does the pear tart. This superb combination of pears and frangipane in a rich pastry shell takes a little longer than a simple flan to prepare but you can do it at your leisure, and the compliments that will greet its appearance will make all the effort worthwhile. Because most of the preparation is done either on the day before or in the morning before you leave, the meal can be served within half an hour of your return – even sooner if you are all quite ravenous.

Warm Welcome

If it is really cold, a spicy Glühwein will provide a warming welcome. Make it in the morning to give the flavours time to develop.

Thick Bean Soup

Metric/Imperial

250 g/8 oz haricot beans, soaked overnight
3 tablespoons olive oil
1 onion, chopped
1 clove garlic, peeled and crushed
1 stick celery, chopped
2 leeks, thinly sliced
500 g/1 lb green cabbage, finely shredded
1 sprig each of fresh thyme and rosemary
1 tablespoon tomato paste
salt
freshly ground black pepper
2 tablespoons chopped fresh parsley
1 large slice bread, cut into 3 mm/1/8 inch dice and lightly browned in the oven, to serve

1. Drain the beans and place in a saucepan. Add 1.75 litres/3 pints cold water, bring to the boil. Boil for 10 minutes, cover, and simmer for about 3 hours or until tender.
2. When the beans are nearly cooked, heat the oil in a large saucepan, add the onion, garlic, and celery and fry gently for 10 minutes. Add the leeks, cabbage and herbs and stir for 3 to 4 minutes.

3. Drain the beans and add the liquor to the vegetables together with the tomato paste and salt and pepper to taste. Bring to the boil and simmer for about 30 minutes. Add the beans, with more water as necessary. Simmer until all the vegetables are tender.
4. Remove the herbs and stir in the parsley. Serve with the browned croûtons. ·11·

Tomato Salad

Metric/Imperial
500 g/1 lb tomatoes, skinned and sliced
3 tablespoons fresh orange juice
½ teaspoon salt
freshly ground black pepper
1 teaspoon chopped fresh parsley
1 tablespoon chopped onion

1. Arrange the tomatoes in a shallow serving dish. Sprinkle them with the orange juice, salt, pepper, parsley and onion.
2. Chill for 15 minutes before serving. ·1·15·

Endive Salad

Metric/Imperial
3 small head endive
1 clove garlic, peeled and crushed
6 tablespoons vinegar
3 tablespoons ground almonds
12 tablespoons olive oil

1. Separate the endive leaves and cut into small strips. Place in a sieve, rinse and drain thoroughly. Place in a serving bowl.
2. Beat the garlic with the vinegar, almonds, and olive oil. Pour over the salad and toss to mix.
3. Cover and leave to stand in the refrigerator for at least 30 minutes before serving. ·2·3·13·

Thick bean soup

Cheese and Chive Bread

Metric/Imperial
250 g/8 oz plain flour
1 teaspoon salt
2 teaspoons dry mustard
4 teaspoons baking powder
250 g/8 oz wholewheat flour
125 g/4 oz butter or margarine
250 g/8 oz cheese, finely grated
1 onion, finely chopped
1 tablespoon chopped fresh chives
2 eggs, lightly beaten
150 ml/¼ pint milk
1 egg, to glaze

1. In a mixing bowl, sift the plain flour, salt, mustard and baking powder. Add the wholewheat flour and rub in the butter or margarine until the mixture resembles fine breadcrumbs. Add the cheese, onion and chives and mix well. Add the eggs and milk and mix to a soft dough.
2. Shape into a large round and score the top into 8 wedges. Transfer to a greased baking sheet and brush with the beaten egg. Place in a preheated oven (190°C/375°F), Gas Mark 5, for about 1 hour, until well risen and golden brown.
3. Transfer to a wire rack to cool. Cut into wedges and serve buttered. ·3·

Cook's Tip:
Any hard cheese can be used in this bread dough. Use a vegetarian Cheddar-type cheese or Cotswold (omit the fresh chives), Lancashire or Cheshire.

If time is at a premium make a quick cheese bread. Beat together 50 g/2 oz butter or margarine, 50 g/2 oz grated Cheddar cheese and 1 peeled and crushed clove garlic. Thickly slice 1 small French stick and spread with the 'cheese butter'. Wrap in foil and bake in a preheated oven (200°C/400°F), Gas Mark 6 for 20 to 25 minutes. Remove the foil and serve immediately.

Pear Tart Frangipane

Metric/Imperial
250 g/8 oz plain flour
150 g/5 oz butter or margarine
1 tablespoon caster sugar
1 egg yolk
1 to 2 tablespoons cold water
Frangipane Filling:
75 g/3 oz butter or margarine
75 g/3 oz caster sugar
1 egg, beaten
75 g/3 oz ground almonds
25 g/1 oz plain flour, sifted
Topping:
3 small pears
1 to 2 teaspoons icing sugar

1. Sift the flour into a bowl. Rub in the butter or margarine. Stir in the sugar and the egg yolk and enough water to mix to a fairly stiff dough. Turn the dough onto a floured surface, knead lightly until smooth, then roll out thinly and use to line a 20 cm/8 inch flan ring placed on a baking sheet.
2. Cream the butter or margarine and sugar together until light and fluffy, then beat in the egg thoroughly. Fold in the ground almonds and flour. Spoon the filling into the flan case and smooth the surface with a palette knife.
3. Peel, halve and core the pears and cut each half across into thin slices. Slide a palette knife under the sliced pear halves and lay them on top of the filling, sliding the slices slightly apart, and arranging them so they radiate from the centre. Press the slices down slightly into the filling. Sift icing sugar lightly over the top.
4. Bake in a preheated oven (200°C/400°F), Gas Mark 6, for 20 minutes, then lower the temperature to 190°C/375°F, Gas Mark 5, and bake for a further 15 to 20 minutes until golden brown and firm in the centre. Cool on a wire rack. ·1·3·10·

C · O · U · N · T · D · O · W · N

Two days before:
Soak the beans for the soup.
The day before:
Cook the beans (see stage 1). Drain, reserving the cooking liquid. Cover and refrigerate. Prepare the pastry for the pear tart and refrigerate.
On the day:
Finish the soup. Prepare, but do not dress, both salads. Cover with cling film and keep in the refrigerator. Make the dressing for the Endive Salad and store, covered, in a cool place. Make the Cheese and Chive Bread and leave on a wire rack to cool. Make and bake the Pear Tart Frangipane. Cover lightly and keep at cool room temperature. Make the Glühwein, if serving. Heat it on your return home.
To serve at 8.00 pm:
7.30: Preheat the oven to (160°C/325°F), Gas Mark 3. Reheat the soup gently. Dress and toss both salads; keep covered in the refrigerator.
7.45: Wrap the bread in foil and reheat.
7.55: Wrap the pear tart in foil and place it in the oven to warm while you eat the soup and salads.
8.00: Serve the meal.

F · R · E · E · Z · E · R · N · O · T · E · S

Thick Bean Soup: Make the soup, cool and freeze. Thaw overnight in the refrigerator.
Cheese and Chive Bread: Wrap in cling film, overwrap in a polythene bag, seal, label and freeze. Thaw overnight at cool room temperature.
Pear Tart Frangipane: Open freeze the cooked tart; wrap in foil. Unwrap, thaw at cool room temperature for 2-3 hours.
Cook's Tip:
Serve the Pear Tart Frangipane with a hot apricot sauce if liked. Simply soak 250 g/8 oz dried apricots overnight in 450 ml/¾ pint water. Simmer the apricots and their soaking liquid for 15 minutes with the juice of ½ lemon and 75 g/3oz caster sugar. Cool slightly, then purée in a blender or food processor.

M·E·N·U

·5·

Teenage Lunch Party for 8

Stuffed Spanish Onions
Garlic Spaghetti
Braised Sorrel
Lettuce and Orange Salad with
Butter and Almond Dressing
•
Meringue Glacé

Today's teenagers are highly health-conscious and even non-vegetarians will appreciate this tasty and well-balanced lunch menu. The pasta dish is tops for both taste and eye-appeal, and has the added bonus that it is extremely inexpensive to prepare, as are the Stuffed Spanish Onions that accompany it.

Side dishes include Braised Sorrel, with its interesting sweet and sour flavour and, for colour contrast, a bright lettuce and orange salad with the crunch of almonds.

Take It Easy

Preparing the meal is simplicity itself. The only dish that makes demands upon the cook is the dessert – a glorious concoction of meringue and ice cream – but as this can, indeed must, be made ahead, it requires nothing more than decoration on the day.

Drinking Partners

What you serve to drink depends upon a lot of factors, not least your natural choice and theirs. A fruit punch may be regarded as passé, so why not play it straight and serve sparkling mineral water with slices of lemon.

Stuffed Spanish Onions

Metric/Imperial
4 large Spanish onions, peeled and halved
salt
50 g/2 oz butter or margarine
6 tomatoes, skinned and chopped
500 g/1 lb button mushrooms, sliced
2 tablespoons chopped fresh parsley
4 tablespoons grated Parmesan cheese
freshly ground black pepper
1 to 2 teaspoons dried oregano

1. Scoop a hollow in the centre of each onion half with a teaspoon, reserving the scooped out onion. Place the halves in a pan, cover with water. Add a little salt, bring to the boil and cook for about 15 minutes, until almost tender. Drain well and set aside.
2. Meanwhile, chop the reserved onion. Melt half of the butter or margarine in a pan and fry the onion for 4 to 5 minutes. Add the tomatoes and mushrooms and cook for a further 2 to 3 minutes.
3. Remove the pan from the heat, stir in the parsley and cheese and season to taste with salt, pepper and oregano.
4. Fill the onion halves with this mixture and dot with the remaining butter. Place in a greased ovenproof dish. Cook in a preheated oven (220°C/425°F), Gas Mark 7, for 12 to 15 minutes or until golden brown and tender. ·8·

Cook's Tip:
If you have a microwave oven, cooking the onions is simplicity itself. Place the stuffed onions on a large microwave plate. Cover loosely with cling film and cook for 3 to 5 minutes on full power.

If you are serving the spaghetti to fussy eaters you may prefer to omit the capers and add 2 tablespoons of chopped fresh parsley.

You can also treat other types of pasta in this way; try tagliatelle, vermicelli or rigatoni.

Garlic Spaghetti

Metric/Imperial
750 g/1½ lb spaghetti
salt
4 tablespoons olive oil
3 cloves garlic, peeled and lightly crushed
25 g/1 oz butter or margarine
2 to 3 tablespoons capers
2 teaspoons chopped fresh basil

1. Cook the spaghetti in boiling salted water until just tender, according to the packet instructions.
2. Meanwhile, heat the oil and garlic in a frying pan and fry until the garlic is golden. Add the butter or margarine and heat until melted. Remove from the heat and add the capers and salt to taste.
3. Drain the spaghetti and place in a large warmed serving dish. Stir in the garlic and caper sauce, with the basil. Toss well and serve immediately. ·8·14·

Braised Sorrel

Metric/Imperial
350 g/12 oz sorrel
350 g/12 oz spinach
15 g/½ oz butter or margarine
pinch of grated nutmeg
4 tablespoons stock
salt
1 tablespoon cream

1. Sort the sorrel and spinach, place in a sieve, rinse and drain thoroughly. Melt the butter or margarine in a pan. Add the sorrel and spinach and cook over a low heat for about 5 minutes.
2. Add the nutmeg, stock and seasoning. Cook for a further 5 to 8 minutes. Stir in the cream and serve immediately. ·8·14·

Stuffed Spanish onions; Garlic spaghetti

Lettuce and Orange Salad with Butter and Almond Dressing

Metric/Imperial

1 Webb's Wonderful or other crisp lettuce
2 oranges
125 g/4 oz butter
50 g/2 oz blanched slivered almonds
1 tablespoon lemon juice
salt
freshly ground black pepper

1. Tear the lettuce into pieces and place in a salad bowl.
2. Remove the peel and pith from the oranges and cut the flesh into segments between the membranes. Add the orange segments to the lettuce and squeeze any orange juice over the top.
3. Melt the butter in a saucepan. Fry the almonds, stirring, until golden brown; about 3 minutes.
4. Allow the almonds to cool slightly, then stir the lemon juice, salt and pepper into the pan.
5. Pour the still warm dressing over the lettuce and the orange segments and toss until well coated. Serve immediately. ·14·

Meringue Glacé

Metric/Imperial
Raspberry Ice Cream:
350 g/12 oz raspberries
2 egg whites
75 g/3 oz caster sugar
300 ml/½ pint double cream
Meringues:
3 egg whites
175 g/6 oz caster sugar
Filling:
250 ml/8 fl oz double cream
1 tablespoon icing sugar
175 g/6 oz raspberries
To Serve:
3 tablespoons double cream, whipped
8 raspberries

1. Line 3 baking sheets with non-stick silicone paper. Draw three 15 cm/6 inch circles.
2. To make the ice cream: purée the raspberries until smooth, then sieve to remove the pips.
3. Whisk the egg whites until stiff, then whisk in the sugar 1 tablespoon at a time. Continue whisking until the meringue is very stiff and holds its shape.
4. Whip the cream until it will stand in soft peaks, then whisk in the raspberry purée. Fork the raspberry cream into the meringue mixture. Pour into a rigid container, cover and freeze for 2 to 3 hours until half-frozen. Stir well, then freeze until almost solid.
5. To make the meringues: whisk the egg whites until stiff, then whisk in 3 tablespoons of the sugar. Carefully fold in the remaining sugar with a metal spoon. Spoon into a piping bag fitted with a 1 cm/½ inch plain nozzle and pipe into the circles marked on the paper. Bake in a preheated oven (120°C/250°F), Gas Mark ½, for 2 hours or until crisp. Place on a wire rack to cool.
6. To make the filling: lightly whip the cream with the icing sugar, then fold in the raspberries.
7. Line a 20 cm/8 inch cake tin with a layer of raspberry ice cream. Place a meringue round on top and cover with half the raspberry filling. Repeat these layers and top with the third meringue round. Cover and freeze until solid.
8. To serve: unwrap the tin and invert onto a serving plate. Rub with a cloth wrung out in very hot water until the cake drops out. Decorate with piped cream and raspberries. Transfer to the refrigerator 1 hour before serving to soften. Serve chilled. **·8·10·**

C · O · U · N · T · D · O · W · N

Two days before or earlier:
Make the Meringue Glacé. Cover and freeze.
The day before:
Scoop out the onion halves. Cook and drain. Cook the filling. When cool, cover and refrigerate separately. Make the spaghetti sauce. Cool, cover tightly and refrigerate. Segment the oranges for the salad.
On the day:
Fill the onion halves. Dot with butter. Cover loosely and refrigerate. Prepare the lettuce and sorrel and store in a polythene bag in the refrigerator.
To serve at 1.00 pm:
12.15: Turn out Meringue Glacé on to a plate.
12.30: Preheat the oven to (220°C/425°F), Gas Mark 7.
12.40: Bring a large saucepan of salted water to the boil for the spaghetti. Chop the basil for the sauce.
12.45: Start cooking the sorrel and cook the spaghetti. Bake the onions.
12.50: Finish the sorrel. Fry the almonds for the salad dressing and add the remaining ingredients. Gently reheat the spaghetti sauce.
12.55: Add the egg to the sorrel. Take any chilled beverages to the table. As soon as the spaghetti is cooked, drain it and toss with the sauce and the chopped basil. Return to the pan and keep warm.
1.00: Toss the salad and serve the meal.

F · R · E · E · Z · E · R · N · O · T · E · S

Only the Meringue Glacé will freeze.

M·E·N·U

·6·

Picnic Lunch for 4

Peanut Roast
Fresh Lettuce Platter
Radicchio Salad
Minted Courgettes
•
Caramelized Peaches

Vegetarian food is perfect for a picnic. The flavours, fresh, natural and unfussed, are entirely at home in the open air.

Peanut Roast

The basis for our picnic is a nut roast. A few years ago this innocent dish got an unfortunate reputation. Devout meat eaters tended to sneer at it, seeing the nut roast as a strange and somewhat bizarre mixture with the effrontery to masquerade as meat. It got such a bad press that for a while it was dropped from many a menu. Luckily it is now back in favour.

Change of Scene

Although the countdown assumes you'll be braving the elements, the meal would be equally good if served as a patio party. Either way, the fact that so much of the food is prepared in advance will ensure that the cook enjoys it as much as her guests.

Chilled Wines

Summer picnics call for crisp cool wines such as Frascati or Chianti. Serve them well-chilled and have plenty of soft drinks on hand too.

Peanut Roast

Metric/Imperial

250 g/8 oz whole shelled peanuts
50 g/2 oz butter or margarine
2 onions, chopped
1 large tomato, skinned and chopped
2 small dessert apples, peeled and diced
25 g/1 oz oatmeal
1 teaspoon chopped fresh sage
salt
freshly ground black pepper
1 egg
little milk

To Garnish:

tomato slices
cucumber slices
parsley sprigs

1. Grease a 500 g/1 lb loaf tin.
2. Chop, mince or grind the peanuts. Heat the butter or margarine in a pan, add the onions, tomato and apples and fry until softened. Add the peanuts, oatmeal, sage, and salt and pepper to taste. Bind with the egg and just enough milk to give a fairly moist consistency.
3. Press into the prepared tin and cover with greased foil. Place in a preheated oven (180°C/350°F), Gas Mark 4, and cook for 45 minutes to 1 hour.
4. Cool in the tin before turning out. Serve sliced garnished with tomato, cucumber and parsley. ·12·

Fresh Lettuce Platter

Metric/Imperial
1 lettuce
250 g/8 oz tomatoes, sliced
salt
freshly ground black pepper
1 small onion, finely chopped
1 tablespoon finely chopped fresh basil or 1 tablespoon chopped fresh parsley
250 ml/8 fl oz soured cream
basil sprigs, to garnish

1. Remove the outer leaves from the lettuce and keep to one side for garnish. Cut the lettuce heart into wedges. Place in a sieve, rinse and drain.
2. Arrange the lettuce heart in a salad bowl or in individual serving dishes, and surround with the tomato slices. Season the tomato liberally with salt and pepper to taste.
3. To make the dressing, stir the onion and basil or parsley into the soured cream and season with salt to taste. Pour over the lettuce just before serving.
4. Shred the reserved lettuce finely and sprinkle in the centre of the salad. Serve immediately, garnished with basil sprigs.

Fresh lettuce platter; Radicchio salad

Radicchio Salad

Metric/Imperial
1 radicchio
3 to 4 medium tomatoes, cut into wedges
125 g/4 oz Camembert cheese, cubed
1 teaspoon made mustard
120 ml/4 fl oz whipping cream
salt
freshly ground black pepper
3 teaspoons chopped fresh parsley
½ onion, chopped

1. Remove the outer leaves from the radicchio and keep to one side for garnish. Separate the heart, tearing larger leaves into pieces. Place in a sieve, rinse and drain thoroughly. Place in a mixing bowl. Add the tomatoes and cheese and mix well.
2. To make the dressing, beat together the remaining ingredients and pour over the salad. Toss lightly.
3. Line a salad bowl with the reserved radicchio leaves and fill with the salad. ·15·

Minted Courgettes

Metric/Imperial
750 g/1½ lb courgettes
2 teaspoons salt
Dressing:
6 tablespoons olive oil
2 tablespoons lemon juice
2 tablespoons chopped fresh mint
freshly ground black pepper

1. Wash the courgettes and grate coarsely into a colander or sieve. Sprinkle the salt over, shake to distribute the salt evenly and place the colander over a bowl to drain. Leave for 1 hour until the juices have run out. Rinse off the excess salt, drain and pat dry.
2. Combine the dressing ingredients in a screw-top jar. Shake well and pour over the courgettes.

Caramelized Peaches

Metric/Imperial
4 ripe medium peaches, peeled
2 to 3 tablespoons lemon juice
125 g/4 oz granulated sugar
300 ml/½ pint water
50 g/2 oz butter

1. Brush each peach with lemon juice. Place in an ovenproof dish.
2. Dissolve the sugar in 150 ml/¼ pint water, then bring to the boil without stirring and boil until the syrup becomes a light golden caramel.
3. Remove from the heat. Quickly pour on the remaining water and stir over a gentle heat until the caramel has dissolved.
4. Pour over the peaches. Cover with a lid or aluminium foil and cook for 30 to 40 minutes in a preheated oven (200°C/400°F), Gas Mark 6, until the peaches are soft and translucent. Turn the peaches in the syrup once or twice during the cooking time, so that they colour evenly.
5. Carefully lift out the peaches with a slotted spoon and stand upright in a serving dish. Place the syrup in a saucepan and boil until it becomes syrupy, then add the butter in small pieces. Pour over the peaches and leave to cool.

C · O · U · N · T · D · O · W · N

In advance:
Cook and freeze the Peanut Roast, if liked.

The day before:
Make the Peanut Roast. When cool, turn out of the tin, wrap in cling film and refrigerate. Make all the salad dressings. Store the two creamy dressings in sealed containers in the refrigerator and the oil-based dressing at room temperature. Make the Caramelized Peaches and place in a covered bowl in the refrigerator. Freeze ice-packs for cool bags if necessary. If the Peanut Roast has been pre-cooked and frozen, thaw it overnight in the refrigerator before serving.

On the day:
Salt the courgettes, drain and pat dry. Prepare the garnish for the Peanut Roast. Pack in a sealed plastic container in the refrigerator. Prepare the ingredients for the lettuce platter: wrap the washed and drained lettuce in a clean dry tea-towel and pack in a rigid plastic container. Slice the tomatoes and pack them separately. Pop the basil sprigs in a polythene bag. Prepare the outer radicchio leaves in the same way as the lettuce and mix the radicchio heart with the tomatoes and cheese in a sturdy portable container. Refrigerate until required.

Just before you leave:
Prepare cool bags or picnic boxes. Overwrap the Peanut Roast in foil and pack it with its garnish. Pack the ingredients for the lettuce and radicchio salads, including the dressings and garnishes. Finish the courgette salad and pack it for the picnic. Transfer the peaches to a rigid plastic container and add them to the bag or box.

In a basket or bag, pack the biscuits and add a loaf of granary bread, if liked. Don't forget salt and pepper and plenty of paper napkins. Face flannels, dipped in warm water to which a little lemon juice has been added, can be packed in individual sealed polythene bags and will be welcome refreshers. Pack the cutlery and crockery and glassware and don't forget a large bag for any rubbish. If you intend taking any hot drinks, make them and put them in flasks. Alternatively, use a flask as a container for ice. Pack the wines and chilled mineral water – if you haven't space in a cooler, wrap them in damp newspaper. Don't forget the corkscrew!

F · R · E · E · Z · E · R · N · O · T · E · S

Only the Peanut Roast will freeze successfully. Cool, remove from the tin, wrap in cling film and overwrap in foil. Freeze for up to 3 months. Thaw overnight at room temperature.

M·E·N·U

· 7 ·

Cocktail Party for 12

Greek Vine Leaves
Roquefort Puffs
Olives with Dill
Avocado Rolls
Lentil and Spinach Croquettes

If the thought of entertaining more than a handful of people to dinner is too much to contemplate, why not have a cocktail party instead?

Cocktails are evocative of a time when the drinks were all important and any snacks offered were eaten absentmindedly. You can alter the emphasis completely by serving a selection of tasty savouries, all designed to complement cocktails, but not to submit to them.

All the recipes in this menu can be prepared in advance so that they will require the minimum of last minute attention. At this type of party, guests tend to come and go, so prior preparation of food means the hostess can relax and circulate, occasionally pausing to replenish the plates of savouries she has set out on small tables around the room.

Finger Food

Small hot pastries are particularly popular with drinks. Roquefort puffs are especially useful as they can be prepared ahead and stored on baking sheets in the refrigerator. They can be quickly cooked when guests arrive.

Classic cocktails

Drinks are best restricted to ready-mixed classic cocktails and wine or sherry. Allow 3-5 drinks per person. Fruit juices and mineral waters should also be provided for drivers and those who don't enjoy alcohol.

Greek Vine Leaves

Metric/Imperial
1 × 425 g/15 oz can vine leaves
250 ml/8 fl oz oil
1 large onion, finely chopped
¼ fennel bulb, grated
2 cloves garlic, peeled and crushed
300 g/10 oz cooked long-grain brown rice
1 tablespoon chopped fresh dill
1 teaspoon dried oregano
salt
freshly ground black pepper
300 ml/½ pint dry red wine

1. Place the vine leaves in a sieve, rinse and drain thoroughly. Heat 1 tablespoon of the oil in a large frying pan, add the onion, fennel and garlic and fry, stirring constantly, for about 8 to 10 minutes or until golden and cooked.
2. Stir in the rice, dill, oregano and salt and pepper to taste. Spread the mixture evenly over the vine leaves. Fold the long sides of the vine leaves over and roll up securely from the shorter edge to make neat parcels.
3. Mix the remaining oil and the red wine in a pan, add the stuffed vine leaves, cover and cook over a gentle heat for about 20 minutes. Remove with a slotted spoon. Chill to serve. ·**8**·

Cook's Tip:
Stuffed vine leaves make a delicious starter, they will add variety to any buffet table spread or, with fresh crusty bread, they make a tasty supper dish.

In Greece, where this dish originated, these stuffed vine leaves are called *dolmas* and are made with a variety of sweet and savoury fillings. You can, for example, replace the stuffing with a mixture of currants, pine nuts and cooked couscous.

Any mixture of herbs may be used in the vine leaves. Try fresh coriander, mint or parsley. Chopped watercress would also give an interesting variation.

Roquefort Puffs

Metric/Imperial
250 g/8 oz puff pastry
250 g/8 oz Roquefort or blue cheeese
1 egg, beaten

1. Roll out the pastry on a lightly floured board to a rectangle about 30 × 25 cm/12 × 10 inch. Cut in half lengthwise, so you have two pieces of pastry 30 × 12.5 cm/12 × 5 inch.
2. Cut the cheese into 16 thin fingers, about 5 cm/2 inches long. Lay two rows of cheese, consisting of eight sticks, along the length of the pastry leaving an equal space between each. Brush around each stick of cheese with a little water.
3. Lay the second sheet of pastry over the top and press down well between each piece of cheese. Cut between the cheese into fingers about 4 cm/1½ inch wide and 6 cm/2½ inch long. Place on a baking sheet and brush with beaten egg. Chill.
4. Bake in a preheated oven (200°C/400°F), Gas Mark 6, for 15 to 20 minutes until golden. Serve hot.

Olives with Dill

Metric/Imperial
1 kg/2 lb large green olives
3 cloves garlic, peeled and crushed
2 red chilli peppers
3 sprigs fresh dill or 1 teaspoon dried
1 bay leaf
120 ml/4 fl oz olive oil
4 tablespoons vinegar

1. Drain the olives. Break the surface or until the stones show. Combine with the remaining ingredients, cover and stand for a day in a cool place. Pack in jars, seal and refrigerate.

Greek vine leaves

Avocado Rolls

Metric/Imperial
2 large avocados
125 g/4 oz cashew or pistachio nuts, finely chopped
500 g/1 lb full fat cream cheese, softened
50 g/2 oz Cheddar cheese, grated
2 teaspoons fresh lime or lemon juice
1 clove garlic, peeled and crushed
½ teaspoon salt
few drops Tabasco sauce
paprika pepper
50 g/2 oz peanuts, finely chopped
croûtons, to serve

1. Peel and stone the avocados and mash with a fork. Combine the avocados with the remaining ingredients except the paprika, nuts and croûtons. Cover and chill for 30 minutes.
2. Halve the mixture and shape each half into a thick cylinder, about 4 cm/1½ inch in diameter. Roll the cylinders in the paprika then the nuts and wrap in foil. Chill for at least two hours. Cut into slices and serve on crisp croûtons of bread.

Lentil and Spinach Croquettes

Metric/Imperial
125 g/4 oz red lentils
500 g/1 lb fresh spinach
175 g/6 oz fresh wholemeal breadcrumbs
1 egg
½ teaspoon grated nutmeg
salt
freshly ground black pepper
oil for shallow frying
To Coat:
beaten egg
breadcrumbs

1. Cover the lentils with water and simmer for about 20 minutes until tender, drain well.
2. Cook the spinach in lightly salted water for 5 to 10 minutes, drain well and chop finely.
3. Mix the lentils, spinach, breadcrumbs, egg, nutmeg and seasoning and form into 24 croquettes. Coat in egg and crumbs and fry until golden.

C · O · U · N · T · D · O · W · N

The day before:
Prepare the vine leaves and cook as directed. Refrigerate. Prepare the Roquefort Puffs to the end of stage 3. Leave on the baking sheet, cover loosely with cling film and refrigerate. Make the Olives with Dill. Cover and leave in a cool place. Make the croûtons. Prepare the Lentil and Spinach Croquettes and coat in breadcrumbs. Refrigerate until required.
On the day:
Make and shape the Avocado Rolls as far as the end of stage 2. Leave in the refrigerator until required. Shallow fry the croquettes. Drain well and place in single layers on baking sheets. Cover and keep cool.
For guests arriving at 8.00 pm:
6.00: Chill white wines; open red wines.
7.00: Preheat the oven to (200°C/400°F) Gas Mark 6. Set out all the ingredients for the cocktails.
7.45: Place one batch of Roquefort Puffs in the oven to cook. Arrange a few croquettes on a small baking sheet. Cover with foil and put in the oven to heat through. Make the first batch of cocktails.
8.00: Slice a few Avocado Rolls and arrange on croûtons. Place on plates, with vine leaves.

F · R · E · E · Z · E · R · N · O · T · E · S

Roquefort Puffs: Make the puffs up to the end of stage 3. Open freeze, then pack in containers. Thaw overnight in the refrigerator.
Lentil and Spinach Croquettes: Prepare to the end of stage 3. Open freeze on baking sheets, then pack, interleaved with squares of freezer-wrap, in rigid plastic boxes. Thaw overnight in the refrigerator.

M·E·N·U

· 8 ·

Elegant Dinner for 8

Crispy Fried Vegetables with
Garlic Mayonnaise

•

Stuffed Artichokes
Fresh Tomato Sauce
Sugar Brown Potatoes
Creamed Runner Beans

•

Iced Lime Soufflé
Blackcurrant Sauce

Some of today's most elegant dinner parties are those where vegetarian food is served exclusively. Thanks to a new breed of superb vegetarian cooks, even the sceptics have had to concede that a vegetarian meal can be magnificent. So never apologise for serving a meatless meal but instead use the opportunity to impress your friends with the versatility of vegetarian cuisine.

Conventional Pattern

Assuming that some of your guests will be non-vegetarians, this menu sticks to the conventional three-course pattern with which they will be most familiar. As a starter there is a selection of vegetables, coated in a featherlight batter and then deep-fried and served with a garlic mayonnaise. Globe artichokes are the main attraction. Stuffed and braised in wine with a tasty tomato sauce, they are sensational. The meal should be accompanied by a clean fruity white wine such as an Alsace Sylvaner, or a Muscadet.

Crispy Fried Vegetables with Garlic Mayonnaise

Metric/Imperial
500 g/1 lb vegetables (see below)
Batter:
2 eggs, separated
300 ml/½ pint pale ale
25 g/1 oz butter or margarine, melted
175 g/6 oz plain wholemeal flour
1 teaspoon dry mustard
pinch ground nutmeg
salt
freshly ground black pepper
oil for deep-frying
Garlic mayonnaise:
150 ml/¼ pint mayonnaise
2 tablespoons double cream
2 cloves garlic, peeled and crushed
1 tablespoon chopped fresh parsley
grated rind of 1 lemon

1. A variety of vegetables can be used for this recipe, including aubergine, celeriac, courgettes, cauliflower florets, Jerusalem artichokes, fennel, mushrooms, parsnip, etc. Use courgettes and mushrooms raw; steam or boil the others until half cooked. Cut into pieces the size of medium mushrooms.
2. To make the batter: mix the egg yolks and beer together, add the butter or margarine and beat until smooth. Sift the flour, mustard and nutmeg into a bowl and gradually beat in the egg mixture, adding salt and pepper to taste. Whisk the egg whites until very stiff, then fold into the batter. Mix the mayonnaise ingredients together.
3. Dip each piece of vegetable into the batter, making sure it is completely coated, and fry in hot oil until golden brown and crisp. Drain on absorbent kitchen paper and serve at once, with the mayonnaise served separately as a dip. ·2·

Iced Lime Soufflé

Stuffed Artichokes

Metric/Imperial
8 large globe artichokes
50 g/2 oz butter or margarine
6 tablespoons oil
1 small onion, finely chopped
8 mushrooms, sliced
few small cauliflower florets
4 tablespoons wholewheat breadcrumbs
2 tablespoons chopped fresh parsley
salt
freshly ground black pepper
12 tablespoons dry white wine

1. Cut off the stalks and trim the bases of the artichokes so that they stand upright. Pull off the coarse outer leaves and cut off the top third of the remaining leaves which are inedible. Pull the leaves back and remove the hairy 'choke' in the centre.

2. Heat the butter or margarine and 1 tablespoon of the oil in a small saucepan, add the onion, mushrooms and cauliflower and fry gently for 5 minutes, stirring frequently. Stir in the breadcrumbs, parsley, and salt and pepper to taste. Fill the artichokes with this mixture.
3. Heat the rest of the oil in a large pan. Stand the artichokes side by side in the pan. Add the wine, cover tightly and simmer over a very low heat for 40 minutes to 1 hour, until tender. (An outer leaf should pull out easily when the artichokes are cooked). Serve with Fresh Tomato Sauce. ·14·

Fresh Tomato Sauce

Metric/Imperial
1 tablespoon olive oil
1 large onion, finely chopped
3 cloves garlic, peeled and thinly sliced
1 × 397 g/14 oz can tomatoes
150 ml/¼ pint dry white wine
2 tablespoons chopped fresh herbs
salt
freshly ground black pepper

1. Heat the oil in a pan, add the onion and garlic and fry gently for approximately 10 minutes until translucent.
2. Stir in the tomatoes with their juice and remaining sauce ingredients, adding salt and pepper to taste. Bring to the boil. Lower the heat, cover and simmer for 30 minutes.
2. Remove lid, increase the heat and cook rapidly for a further 2 minutes.

Variation:
This delicious sauce is perfect for most green vegatables. Broccoli, French beans, courgettes or even cucumber would be excellent alternatives. The cooking time in Stage 2 may vary slightly. The vegetables should be simmered until just tender. Take care not to over cook.

Sugar Brown Potatoes

Metric/Imperial
1 kg/2 lb small new potatoes
salt
125 g/4 oz soft brown sugar
125 g/4 oz butter

1. Cook the potatoes in boiling, salted water until just tender. Drain and keep warm.
2. Place the sugar in a heavy-based pan and heat very slowly, stirring constantly, until the sugar has melted and is light brown in colour.
3. Stir in the butter. When it has melted, add the potatoes and toss carefully until evenly coated.

Creamed Runner Beans

Metric/Imperial
1 kg/2 lb runner beans
50 g/2 oz butter or margarine
1 onion, finely chopped
2 cloves garlic, peeled and crushed
300 ml/½ pint soured cream or double cream
salt
freshly ground black pepper
1½ tablespoons chopped fresh parsley, to garnish

1. Melt the butter or margarine in a pan, add the onion and garlic and fry gently for 5 minutes.
2. Plunge the beans into a separate pan of boiling salted water, bring back to the boil and simmer for 3 minutes.
3. Drain the beans and add to the onion with the cream. Fold gently to mix, add the herbs and salt and pepper to taste, then cook gently for 3 to 4 minutes until the beans are tender. (Do not let the mixture boil or the cream may separate).
3. Spoon the mixture into a warmed serving dish, sprinkle with the chopped parsley or chives and serve immediately. ·14·

Iced Lime Soufflé

Metric/Imperial
finely grated rind of 3 limes
juice of 4 limes
4 eggs, separated
175 g/6 oz light soft brown sugar
300 ml/½ pint double cream
To Serve:
6 tablespoons double cream, whipped
½ lime, thinly sliced

1. Tie a double band of foil around a 900 ml/1½ pint soufflé dish to stand at least 5 cm/2 inches above the rim.
2. Put the lime rind in a bowl with the egg yolks and 125 g/4 oz sugar and whisk until thick and mousse-like. Heat the lime juice in a small pan, pour over the egg mixture and whisk until thoroughly incorporated.
3. Whisk the egg whites until stiff, then gradually whisk in remaining sugar. Whip the cream until it will stand in soft peaks, then fold into the lime mixture. Fold in the egg whites. Spoon into the dish and level the surface. Open freeze.
4. To serve: remove the paper, then decorate with whipped cream and lime slices. Transfer to refrigerator 30 minutes before serving to soften. Serve with Blackcurrant Sauce.

Blackcurrant Sauce

Metric/Imperial
250 g/8 oz blackcurrants
125 g/4 oz granulated sugar
250 ml/8 fl oz water

1. Top and tail the blackcurrants and put them in a pan with the sugar and water. Bring slowly to the boil, lower the heat and simmer for about 5 minutes.
2. Cool, purée and sieve. Serve chilled.

C · O · U · N · T · D · O · W · N

A few days before:
Make the Iced Lime Soufflé. Open freeze then wrap in cling film. Make the Blackcurrant Sauce. Cool, cover and refrigerate. Make the Fresh Tomato Sauce and refrigerate.
The day before:
Make the garlic mayonnaise. Cover closely and store in the refrigerator. Make the batter mixture but do not add the egg whites. Cover and keep in a cool place. Prepare the artichokes for filling, wrap them individually in cling film and keep in a cool place. Make the filling. Cool, cover and refrigerate. Make the sauce for the runner beans, cover and refrigerate. Cook the beans until just tender. Drain and cover.
On the day:
Prepare the vegetables for frying. Fill the artichokes.
To serve at 8.00 pm:
6.00: Chill the white wines.
7.00: Finish the artichokes and begin cooking.
7.15: Boil the potatoes, drain well and set aside. Finish the batter and set it aside.
7.30: Put the tomato sauce on to reheat. Fold together the runner beans and sauce and set over a low heat. Begin browning the potatoes. Preheat the oven to (140°C/275°F), Gas Mark 1.
7.40: Stir the batter gently. Begin dipping and frying the vegetables. Place on baking sheets lined with absorbent kitchen paper to drain and keep each batch warm in the oven while cooking the next.
7.50: Decorate the soufflé. Transfer to the refrigerator to soften.
8.00: Place the wines on the table. Serve the meal.

F · R · E · E · Z · E · R · N · O · T · E · S

Fresh Tomato Sauce: Cool, pack into rigid plastic container, leaving headroom, seal and label. Freeze for up to 12 months. Thaw overnight at cool room temperature.
Blackcurrant Sauce: Pack as the tomato sauce. Freeze for up to 12 months. Thaw overnight.

MENU

· 9 ·

Pasta Lunch for 4

Pasta with Beans
Cheese and Onion Ring
Herby Green Salad
•
Ginger Ice Cream

The problem with today's family is that it tends to explode in all directions, especially on Saturdays. There are sports fixtures, shopping expeditions, fishing trips, computer clubs – it's tough enough trying to remember who wants picking up when and where without having to cope with cooking a mammoth meal as well.

However, Saturday is also the start of the weekend, the time when students come home to get their washing done and house guests arrive with hearty appetites.

Simple Yet Substantial

What you need is a menu for a simple yet substantial meal that can be prepared in advance and assembled with little effort and less time; that will wait if you're late and stretch if it must.

Here it is – the elastic lunch. We've done all the planning for you so that in just 45 minutes you can produce a memorable meal.

Two-way Stretch

If extra guests pitch up unexpectedly you can happily extend the pasta dish. It will accept up to 175 g/6 oz extra macaroni, and you can also add more vegetables to the sauce together with additional liquid.

Pasta with Beans

Metric/Imperial
175 g/6 oz haricot beans
1 litre/1¾ pints cold water
1½ teaspoons salt
500 g/1 lb wholewheat macaroni
2 tablespoons olive oil
1 large onion, chopped
2 large carrots, sliced
4 celery sticks, chopped
1 clove garlic, peeled and crushed
500 g/1 lb tomatoes, skinned and chopped
1 teaspoon chopped fresh sage
1 teaspoon chopped fresh marjoram
salt
¼ teaspoon freshly ground black pepper
To Serve:
chopped fresh parsley
grated Parmesan cheese

1. In a large bowl combine the beans with the water and salt and refrigerate overnight. Next day, transfer to a large saucepan. Bring to the boil, boil for 10 minutes. Reduce the heat and simmer, covered, for 1 to 2 hours, or until the beans are tender. Drain and reserve 600 ml/1 pint of liquid.
2. Cook the macaroni in boiling salted water until 'al dente', drain.
3. In a large, heavy-based pan heat the oil and sauté the onion, carrots, celery and garlic until soft. Add the tomatoes, sage, marjoram, salt and pepper. Cover and cook over a gentle heat for 20 minutes.
4. In a large saucepan combine the beans, macaroni and tomato mixture. Add 350 ml/12 fl oz of the bean liquid. Bring to the boil, cover and simmer for 15 to 20 minutes, stirring occasionally and adding more bean liquid if necessary. Season to taste.
6. Turn into a serving bowl or casserole. Sprinkle with chopped parsley and Parmesan cheese and serve hot. ·3·13·

Cheese and Onion Ring

Metric/Imperial
175 g/6 oz Double Gloucester cheese, grated
½ teaspoon dried mixed herbs
2 onions, finely chopped
pinch dry mustard
2 tablespoons mild mustard pickle
salt
freshly ground black pepper
1 × 398 g/14 oz packet frozen shortcrust pastry, thawed
beaten egg, to glaze
poppy seeds or cracked wheat, to sprinkle

1. In a bowl, mix the cheese with the herbs, onion, mustard, mustard pickle and salt and pepper to taste, blending together well.
2. Roll out the pastry on a light floured surface to a rectangle measuring approximately 40 × 28 cm/16 × 11 inches.
3. Spread the cheese filling over the pastry with a spatula to within 1 cm/½ inch of the edges. Brush one long edge with beaten egg to glaze. Roll up from the opposite long edge, like a Swiss roll. Press firmly along the glazed edge to seal. Place seam-side down on a greased baking sheet.
4. Using scissors, snip across the long edge of the roll at 2.5 cm/1 inch intervals, almost through to the other edge. Shape the roll into a ring, brush the ends with beaten egg to glaze and press together to seal firmly.
5. Carefully lift each cut section of the ring and tilt slightly sideways so that the filling is just exposed. Brush the ring with beaten egg and sprinkle with poppy seeds or cracked wheat.
6. Place in a preheated oven (200°C/400°F), Gas Mark 6 and cook for 30 to 35 minutes or until golden brown and cooked through. Allow to cool slightly on a wire rack. Serve the ring warm.

Herby green salad

Herby Green Salad

Metric/Imperial

1 clove garlic, peeled and chopped
1 cos lettuce
125 g/4 oz lamb's lettuce
1 bunch watercress
1 punnet mustard and cress
1 bunch chives
1 bunch parsley
1 bunch basil
1 bunch mint
2 oranges, peeled, sliced and quartered
Dressing:
2 tablespoons olive oil
1 tablespoon wine vinegar
1 tablespoon lemon juice
2 cloves garlic, peeled and crushed
1 teaspoon brown sugar
1 teaspoon tarragon mustard

1. Use the cut clove garlic to rub round the inside of a large salad bowl, then discard.
2. Wash and prepare the salad greens. Chop the chives and parsley and strip the leaves from the basil and mint, discarding the stems.
3. Place the salad greens and herbs in the salad bowl with the orange pieces. Combine the dressing ingredients in a screw-top jar. Shake well and toss into the salad just before serving. ·1·2·13·

Ginger Ice Cream

Metric/Imperial

2 eggs
2 egg yolks
75 g/3 oz sugar
450 ml/¾ pint single cream
1 teaspoon vanilla essence
200 ml/7 fl oz double cream, lightly whipped
50 g/2 oz preserved ginger, chopped
1 tablespoon preserved ginger syrup

1. Beat the eggs, egg yolks and sugar until smooth and thick.
2. Heat the single cream to just under boiling point, then pour it on to the egg mixture, beating all the time.
3. Strain the mixture into the top of a double boiler or into a heatproof bowl placed over a pan of simmering water and stir the mixture over a gentle heat until it is thick enough to coat the back of a wooden spoon – about 20 minutes. Cool.
4. Fold in the vanilla essence, lightly whipped cream, chopped ginger and ginger syrup. Pour the mixture into a freezer container and freeze for 2 hours. Beat the ice cream at 30 minute intervals during freezing bringing the ice cream at the sides into the middle. ·1·

Cook's Tip:
The Ginger Ice Cream is excellent served with a warm orange compote. Simply place 600 ml/1 pint of orange juice, 2 cinnamon sticks and 125 g/4 oz soft brown sugar in a small pan. Heat gently, stirring, until the sugar dissolves. Bring to the boil and boil for 2 minutes. Peel and chop 3 oranges and 2 bananas and place in a serving dish. Pour over the warm syrup and serve with the ice cream.

C · O · U · N · T · D · O · W · N

Two days before:
Make the bean dish: combine the beans with the water and salt and refrigerate overnight. Make the Ginger Ice Cream.

The day before:
Cook the beans. Drain, reserving the cooking liquid. Cool, cover and refrigerate. Cook the macaroni, drain, cool, cover and refrigerate. Prepare the vegetable sauce for the pasta. Cool, cover and refrigerate. Make the Cheese and Onion Ring to the end of stage 5. Cover loosely with cling film and refrigerate. Prepare the oranges for the green salad. Cover and keep cool. Make the salad dressing. Cover and set aside at cool room temperature. If any dishes have been frozen, thaw them as directed.

On the day:
To serve at 1.00 pm:
12.15: Preheat the oven to (200°C/400°F), Gas Mark 6.
12.25: Finish the pasta dish. In a large saucepan combine the beans, macaroni and vegetable sauce. Add the reserved bean liquid. Bring to the boil, reduce the heat and simmer.
12.30: Place the Cheese and Onion Ring in the oven to cook. Wash the salad greens and place all the ingredients except the dressing in the salad bowl. Chop the parsley for the pasta garnish.
12.45: Stir the pasta mixture. Transfer the ice cream to the refrigerator to soften.
1.00: Reduce the oven temperature to 150°C/300°F, Gas Mark 2. Fix the drinks. Garnish the pasta dish, toss the salad, transfer the Cheese and Onion Ring to a platter and serve the meal.

F · R · E · E · Z · E · R · N · O · T · E · S

Pasta with Beans: Cool, pack, seal and label at the end of stage 4. (Add all the bean liquid). Store for up to 3 months. Thaw overnight at room temperature.
Cheese and Onion Ring: Prepare but do not cook the ring. Open freeze, wrap in cling film, then overwrap in a polythene bag. Seal, label and return to the freezer for up to 3 months. Thaw overnight in the refrigerator.

M·E·N·U

· 10 ·

Celebration Lunch for 6

Spinach Roulade
Buttered Salsify
Sweetcorn Salad
Tomatoes with Basil
•
Gooseberry Crunch
or
Ginger Vacherin

Celebration meals call for special menus. They should be elaborate enough to emphasize the importance of the occasion, yet so organized as to require little attention once the guests have gathered.

Honour the Occasion

This splendid menu fits the bill. The Spinach Roulade is impressive enough to honour any occasion, yet it is surprisingly simple to make. Don't be daunted by the final filling and rolling. It works perfectly and the roulade will keep warm in the oven while you settle your guests.

Just Desserts

To sustain the ambiance of the evening, the dessert should be dramatic. Achieving the desired effect takes time, so the desserts suggested can be prepared and even frozen well in advance of the party.

A meal like this deserves to be accompanied by a superior wine. A Puligny Montrachet or a Pouilly-Fuisse would complement the meal perfectly. And if the celebration calls for Champagne, end on a high note with a glass of Veuve Clicquot.

Spinach Roulade

Metric/Imperial
Roulade:
500 g/1 lb spinach leaves
4 eggs, separated
salt
freshly ground black pepper
Filling:
25 g/1 oz butter or margarine
4 onions, sliced
125 g/4 oz button mushrooms, sliced
25 g/1 oz wholemeal flour
300 ml/½ pint milk
1 tablespoon grated Parmesan cheese

1. Line a 32 × 23 cm/13 × 9 inch roasting pan with oiled greaseproof paper or non-stick parchment so that it comes above the sides of the pan.
2. To make the roulade: wash the spinach thoroughly, then put in a large pan with only the water clinging to the leaves. Cook gently for about 5 minutes until tender, then drain well.
3. Chop the spinach finely, then put in a bowl with the egg yolks and seasonings. Beat well. Whisk the egg whites until stiff, then fold into the spinach mixture. Spoon into the tin and smooth the surface.
4. Bake in a preheated oven (200°C/400°F), Gas Mark 6, for 10 to 15 minutes until the roulade is well risen, firm and just beginning to brown.
5. Meanwhile, make the filling: melt the butter or margarine in a pan. Add the onions and mushrooms and fry gently for 5 minutes
6. Add the flour and cook for 1 to 2 minutes, stirring constantly. Remove from the heat and gradually stir in the milk, beating well after each addition. Return to the heat and simmer until thick and smooth.
7. Sprinkle the Parmesan cheese over a large sheet of greaseproof paper. Turn the roulade out onto the paper, then carefully peel off the lining paper.
8. Spread the sauce over the roulade and roll up.

Gooseberry crunch

Buttered Salsify

Metric/Imperial
2 teaspoons plain wholemeal flour
2 tablespoons lemon juice
1 teaspoon salt
2 to 3 tablespoons water
500 g/1 lb salsify, peeled and cut into 5 cm/2 inch lengths
50 g/2 oz butter
freshly ground black pepper
finely chopped fresh parsley

1. Blend the flour with the lemon juice, salt and water. Strain into a pan of water and bring to the boil, stirring all the time.
2. Add the salsify, cover and cook for about 30 to 40 minutes until tender. Drain well.
3. Melt the butter in a pan, add the salsify and brown lightly. Place in a serving dish and sprinkle with pepper and parsley.

Sweetcorn Salad

Metric/Imperial

500 g/1 lb sweetcorn kernels, fresh, frozen or canned
salt
4 tablespoons corn oil
1 tablespoon wine vinegar
1 tablespoon tomato ketchup
1 tablespoon soft brown sugar
1 tablespoon grated onion
50 g/2 oz raisins
1 red or green pepper, cored, seeded and finely chopped

1. Cook the fresh or frozen sweetcorn kernels in salted boiling water until tender, or according to pack instructions. Drain and leave to cool. If using canned kernels, simply drain.
2. Pour the corn oil into a mixing bowl. Add the vinegar, Worcestershire sauce, tomato ketchup, sugar and grated onion, and mix well.
3. Stir in the raisins and chopped pepper. Add the sweetcorn and stir until well mixed. ·3·4·15·

Tomatoes with Basil

Metric/Imperial

4 to 5 large ripe tomatoes
½ Spanish onion
5 to 6 large basil leaves
1 to 2 tablespoons olive oil
salt
freshly ground black pepper
squeeze of lemon juice

1. Peel the tomatoes, remove the cores and cut into wedges. Finely slice the onion. Shred the basil leaves but do not chop.
2. Combine the tomatoes, onion and basil in a bowl. Drizzle over a little oil, season with salt, a fresh grinding of pepper and a squeeze of lemon juice. Toss lightly before serving. ·4·

Gooseberry Crunch

Metric/Imperial

125 g/4 oz ginger nuts, crushed
50 g/2 oz hazelnuts, chopped and lightly toasted
500 g/1 lb gooseberries
75 g/3 oz demerara sugar
2 heads elderflower, tied in muslin (optional)
1 egg white
50 g/2 oz soft brown sugar
150 ml/¼ pint double cream
6 tablespoons double cream, whipped, to serve

1. Mix together the biscuits and hazelnuts.
2. Put the gooseberries in a pan with the sugar and elderflower (if using). Cover and simmer gently for 15 minutes until tender. Discard the elderflower (if used), then leave the gooseberries to cool. Work in an electric blender or food processor until smooth, then sieve to remove tops and tails.
3. Whisk the egg white until stiff, then gradually whisk in the soft brown sugar. Continue whisking until the mixture stands in stiff peaks. Whip the cream until it will stand in soft peaks. Fold the gooseberry purée into the egg whites with the cream. Place half the fruit mixture in a serving dish and cover with half the biscuit mixture. Repeat the layers then pipe the cream around the edge. ·2·

Ginger Vacherin

Metric/Imperial

5 egg whites
300 g/10 oz soft brown sugar
2 teaspoons ground ginger
450 ml/¾ pint double cream
50 g/2 oz preserved stem ginger, drained and thinly sliced, with 2 tablespoons syrup reserved
To Serve:
4 tablespoons double cream, whipped
8 thin slices preserved stem ginger

1. Line 3 baking sheets with non-stick silicone paper or baking parchment. With a pencil, draw a 20 cm/8 inch circle on each piece of paper.
2. To make the ginger meringue: whisk the egg whites until stiff, then whisk in 3 tablespoons of the sugar with the ground ginger. Carefully fold in the remaining sugar with a metal spoon. Spoon into a piping bag fitted with a 1 cm/½ inch plain nozzle and pipe over the circles marked on the paper.
3. Bake in a preheated oven (110°C/225°F), Gas Mark ¼, for 2 hours until crisp. Peel the paper carefully off the meringue rounds, then place on a wire rack and leave to cool.
4. To make the filling: whip the cream into the ginger syrup until it will stand in soft peaks, then fold in the sliced ginger. Sandwich the meringue rounds together with the ginger and cream filling. ·5·

Rescue Tactic:
If the meringues are broken, crush roughly and fold into the whipped cream and ginger. Cover and freeze until firm. Serve in scoops.

C · O · U · N · T · D · O · W · N

Two days before:
Make the ginger meringue rounds, if planning to serve the Vacherin. Cool and store in an air-tight container.

The day before:
Cook and chop the spinach for the roulade and add the egg yolks, nutmeg and seasoning. Cover the surface of the mixture with cling film and refrigerate. Make the roulade filling. Cool, cover and refrigerate. Prepare the hazelnuts and biscuits for the Gooseberry Crunch, if serving, and combine them in a polythene bag. Store them in a cool place. Cook and purée the gooseberries, if necessary, then cover and refrigerate.

On the day:

To serve at 1.00 pm:
9.00 am: Prepare the greaseproof paper case for the roulade. Cook the salsify and drain well. Cover and keep in a cool place. Chop the parsley for the garnish. Prepare, but do not dress the Tomatoes with Basil. Complete the Sweetcorn Salad, cover and refrigerate. Finish, but do not decorate your chosen dessert. Store in the refrigerator.
11.00: Chill the white wine and the Champagne. Whip the cream to decorate the dessert. Slice the ginger if serving the vacherin.
12.00: Take the roulade mixture out of the refrigerator and allow it to come to room temperature.
12.15: Add the dressing and toss the Tomatoes with Basil. Cover and keep at cool room temperature. Melt the butter, ready to reheat the salsify.
12.25: Preheat the oven to (200°C/400°F), Gas Mark 6.
12.30: Transfer the roulade filling to a small pan and reheat gently. Whisk the egg whites and fold into the roulade mixture. Spoon the mixture into the prepared paper case.
12.40: Bake the roulade. Prepare the greaseproof paper for rolling the roulade. Add the salsify to the butter and reheat.
12.50: Check the roulade. If ready, turn out and roll with the filling. Transfer to a serving dish. Lower the oven temperature to 150°C/300°F, Gas Mark 2, and return the roulade to the oven while you garnish the salsify, set out the wines and seat the guests.
1.00: Serve the meal.
Decorate the dessert just before serving.

F · R · E · E · Z · E · R · N · O · T · E · S

Gooseberry Crunch: Layer the Gooseberry Crunch but do not add the final decoration of piped cream. Open freeze, then cover with cling film and overwrap in a plastic bag. Seal, label and return to the freezer for up to 3 months. Thaw overnight in the refrigerator. Add the cream decoration before serving.
Ginger Vacherin: Make the vacherin but do not add the decoration. Open freeze, then place in a rigid container. Seal, label and store for up to 6 months. Thaw for 4 hours at room temperature. Decorate.

M·E·N·U

· 11 ·

Bonfire Party for 8

Tomato and Stilton Soup
Paprika Soup
•
Ginger Applecake
Nutty Brownies

On a cold November evening nothing lifts the spirits more than inviting a handful of neighbours to share in Bonfire Night celebrations. Gingerbread, parkin and bonfire toffee are the traditional fare, especially in the north of England, but adults will probably prefer something savoury as the fireworks soar and the sparklers sizzle.

Hand-held

The important thing to remember is that the food should be warming, nourishing and easy to hold in gloved hands while your guests stand around the fire. Soup is perfect and we suggest you offer a choice of two. Carefully carry the pots or tureens of soup outside, provide ladles and mugs and invite guests to help themselves. But please be careful when carrying hot soup, especially if the night is frosty. If you have a camp stove you can set up in a safe position not too far from the fire, it might be better to merely warm the soups indoors and then reheat them fully at the point where they will be served.

Afterthoughts

As a finale, Ginger Applecake is scrumptious and can be made very cheaply when apples are plentiful. Nutty Brownies are moist and more-ish, and worth making up in batches to be sure you don't run out.

Tomato and Stilton Soup

Metric/Imperial

50 g/2 oz butter or margarine
2 tablespoons olive oil
2 medium onions, chopped
2 cloves garlic, chopped
2 celery sticks, chopped
1 carrot, chopped
500 g/1 lb tomatoes, skinned and chopped
1 × 397 g/14 oz can tomatoes
900 ml/1½ pints vegetable stock or water
2 tablespoons tomato paste
1 teaspoon sugar
1 teaspoon dried oregano
1 teaspoon salt
150 ml/¼ pint red wine
freshly ground black pepper
To Garnish:
300 ml/½ pint single cream
125 g/4 oz crumbled Stilton cheese
125 g/4 oz croûtons (see Cook's Tip)

1. Heat the butter or margarine and oil in a large saucepan and gently sauté the onion, garlic and celery until soft. Add the carrot and fresh tomatoes and cook together for about 10 minutes, stirring occasionally.
2. Stir in the canned tomatoes and the stock or water together with the tomato paste, sugar, oregano, salt, wine and pepper. Bring to the boil, then reduce the heat and simmer for 1 hour.
3. Allow the soup to cool slightly, then work in an electric blender or food processor and process for about 1 minute, until smooth. If a finer-textured soup is preferred, process again for a further minute. Alternatively, press the soup through a sieve.
4. Return the soup to the saucepan to reheat, taste and adjust the seasoning, if necessary, and serve piping hot with a swirl of cream in each bowl. Garnish with a sprinkling of Stilton or croûtons. ·4·

Cook's Tip:
To make croûtons: cut slices of bread (crusts removed) into tiny cubes. Fry in oil or butter until golden and crisp and then drain on absorbent kitchen paper.

Paprika Soup

Metric/Imperial

2 tablespoons vegetable oil
1 onion, chopped
125 g/4 oz carrots, sliced
125 g/4 oz frozen peas
1 clove garlic, peeled and crushed
2 tablespoons plain flour
1 tablespoon paprika
½ teaspoon caraway seeds (optional)
500 g/1 lb tomatoes, skinned, seeded and roughly chopped
1.5 litres/2½ pints light stock
salt
freshly ground black pepper
1 kg/2 lb potatoes, peeled and cut into small chunks
To Serve:
about 150 ml/¼ pint soured cream
orange slices
fresh coriander sprigs

1. Heat the oil in a large pan, add the onion, carrots, peas and garlic and fry gently for 5 minutes without browning.
2. Lower the heat, sprinkle in the flour, paprika and caraway seeds, if using, and fry for a further 1 minute, stirring. Add the chopped tomatoes, gradually stir in the stock, then bring to the boil. Lower the heat, add salt and pepper to taste, cover and simmer gently for 1 hour.
3. Add the potatoes and simmer for 40 minutes or until the potatoes are just tender. Top with the soured cream and garnish. Serve immediately.

Tomato and stilton soup

Ginger Applecake

Metric/Imperial
175 g/6 oz self-raising flour
1 teaspoon ground ginger
1 teaspoon baking powder
pinch of salt
75 g/3 oz soft brown sugar
1 egg, lightly beaten
6 to 8 tablespoons milk
25 g/1 oz unsalted butter, melted and cooled
Topping:
500 g/1 lb cooking apples
juice of 1 lemon
75 g/3 oz demerara sugar
1 teaspoon ground ginger
50 g/2 oz unsalted butter, melted and cooked

1. Grease a 35 × 20 cm/12 × 8 inch Swiss roll tin.
2. Sift the flour into a bowl with the ginger, baking powder and salt. Stir in the soft brown sugar. Add the egg, 6 tablespoons of the milk and the melted butter and beat to a soft dropping consistency, adding more milk if it is too stiff.
3. Peel, core and slice the apples into thin wedges. Put the apple wedges in a bowl with the lemon juice, demerara sugar and ginger. Fold gently to mix.
4. Spoon the cake mixture into the prepared tin and level the surface. Arrange the apple wedges over the top. Pour over any liquid remaining in the bowl, then drizzle over the melted butter.
5. Bake in a preheated oven (200°C/400°F), Gas Mark 6 for 35 minutes until the apples are golden brown on top. Remove from the oven and cool.

Nutty Brownies

Metric/Imperial
75 g/3 oz plain flour
¼ teaspoon salt
25 g/1 oz cocoa powder
250 g/8 oz caster sugar
125 g/4 oz unsalted butter, softened
2 eggs, beaten
1 teaspoon vanilla essence
75 g/3 oz mixed chopped nuts

1. Grease a 20 cm/8 inch square cake tin, line the base with greaseproof paper and grease the paper.
2. Sift the flour, salt and cocoa powder into a bowl. Stir in the caster sugar. Add the butter, eggs and vanilla essence and beat thoroughly. Fold in the nuts.
3. Turn the mixture into the prepared tin and level the surface. Bake in a preheated moderate oven (180°C/350°F), Gas Mark 4, for 25 minutes or until the top is just firm to the touch. Leave the cake to cool in the tin, then turn out, peel off the lining paper and cut into squares. **Makes 16**

C · O · U · N · T · D · O · W · N

The day before:
Make the soups if necessary. Cool, cover and store in the refrigerator. Make the Nutty Brownies. Cool and store in an airtight tin.
On the day:
Make the Ginger Applecake.
To serve at 8.00 pm:
7.15: Preheat the oven to (180°C/350°F), Gas Mark 4.
7.30: Bring the soups to the boil. Reduce the heat, cover and simmer gently to reheat. Cut up French Bread, if serving. Wrap in foil and place in the oven to warm through. Wrap the applecake in foil and warm it through in the oven. Set out the brownies.
8.00: Serve the soup and accompaniments.

F · R · E · E · Z · E · R N · O · T · E · S

Soups: Cool and pack in rigid containers. Thaw at cool room temperature for 4-5 hours.
Ginger Applecake and Nutty Brownies: When cool, wrap in cling film and freeze. Thaw at cool room temperature for 4-5 hours.

M·E·N·U

· 12 ·

An Indian Feast for 6

Spiced Cauliflower
Mushroom and Nut Pilaff
Dhal
Mixed Vegetable Pickle
Naan Bread
•
Lemon Syllabub
Mixed Melon Salad

There's nothing new about a vegetarian diet. The majority of the peoples of India have been following one for centuries so it is not surprising that the cuisine of that continent includes some of the world's most delicious vegetarian recipes.

Traditional Pattern

Our menu follows the traditional Indian pattern, with a main dish and several side dishes served with rice, leavened bread, chutneys and pickles. Cauliflower takes the leading role, in a crisp textured medium-hot curry which is accompanied by a simple Mushroom and Nut Pilaff. We suggest serving these with a traditional Dhal and a homemade vegetable pickle but any of the conventional sambals would be appropriate: raita, sliced banana, mango chutney or lime pickle.

Ice Cold Drinks

Cold beer is often the preferred drink with Indian food. Alternatively, serve a medium-sweet white wine such as a Californian or South African Chenin Blanc or a Rosé d'Anjou.

Spiced Cauliflower

Metric/Imperial
500 g/1 lb cauliflower florets
To Serve:
2 tablespoons vegetable oil
1 clove garlic, peeled and thinly sliced
1 cm/½ inch piece fresh root ginger, peeled and shredded
2 teaspoons ground coriander
1 teaspoon chilli powder
1 teaspoon ground turmeric
1 teaspoon whole coriander seeds
1 onion, finely chopped
4 carrots, thinly sliced
1 green pepper, cored, seeded and diced
150 ml/¼ pint homemade vegetable stock
salt
150 ml/¼ pint plain yogurt
1 tablespoon chopped fresh coriander

1. Heat the oil in a large frying pan, add the garlic and ginger and fry gently for 2 minutes. Add the spices, stir over low heat for 2 minutes, then add the onion, carrots and green pepper and fry for a further 5 minutes.
2. Increase the heat, add the frozen cauliflower florets, stock and salt to taste. Bring to the boil, lower the heat, cover the pan and simmer gently for about 7 minutes.
3. Stir in the plain yogurt, heat through gently for about 1 minute, stirring, then spoon into a warmed serving dish and sprinkle with the chopped coriander. Serve immediately.

Mushroom and Nut Pilaff

Metric/Imperial
4 tablespoons olive oil
250 g/8 oz brown rice
1 onion, sliced
1 clove garlic, peeled and crushed
2 sticks celery, chopped
1 red pepper, cored, seeded and chopped
1 green pepper, cored, seeded and chopped
175 g/6 oz cashew nuts, chopped
125 g/4 oz button mushrooms, quartered
salt
freshly ground black pepper

1. Heat 2 tablespoons of the oil in a large pan and fry the rice for 2 to 3 minutes. Cover with boiling water and cook for 45 minutes, then drain well.
2. Heat the remaining oil in a large pan and fry the onion until transparent. Add the garlic, celery, peppers, nuts and mushrooms and cook together for 5 to 7 minutes. Add the cooked rice and seasoning and simmer gently, stirring occasionally, until heated through. Serve immediately.

Dhal

Metric/Imperial
1 tablespoon oil
1 onion, finely chopped
1 clove garlic, peeled and crushed
½ teaspoon ground turmeric
1 teaspoon ground coriander
1 teaspoon curry powder
175 g/6 oz red lentils, soaked for 30 minutes and drained
600 ml/1 pint vegetable stock
salt
freshly ground black pepper

1. Heat the oil in a pan and fry the onion until soft. Add the garlic, turmeric, coriander and curry powder and cook for a further 2 minutes over a low heat stirring all the time.
2. Add the red lentils, vegetable stock, salt and freshly ground black pepper to taste, cover and cook gently for about 50 to 60 minutes until the lentils are quite soft. (Dahl should be the consistency of a very thick pea soup).

Spiced cauliflower

Mixed Vegetable Pickle

Metric/Imperial

350 g/12 oz red kidney beans, soaked overnight and drained
4 red peppers, cored, seeded and cut into 5 cm/2 inch pieces
1 medium cauliflower, broken into florets
500 g/1 lb French beans, cut into 5 cm/2 inch lengths
salt
1 × 397 g/14 oz can sweetcorn, drained
1.1 litre/2 pints cider vinegar
175 g/6 oz molasses sugar
3 tablespoons mustard seed
5 tablespoons dry mustard
1 teaspoon ground turmeric

1. Place the kidney beans in a pan, cover with water, bring to the boil and boil for 10 minutes. Simmer for 1 to 1½ hours until just tender, then drain.
2. Blanch the peppers, cauliflower and French beans in boiling salted water for 5 minutes, drain and mix with the kidney beans and corn.
3. Heat the vinegar in a pan with the sugar, mustard seed, dry mustard and turmeric, until the sugar has completely dissolved. Add the vegetables and simmer gently for about 5 minutes. Allow to cool slightly, then ladle the pickle into warmed, sterilised, preserving jars. Seal, label and store in a cool dry place. **Makes 1.75 kg/3½ lb**

Naan Bread

Metric/Imperial

250 g/8 oz plain flour
½ teaspoon baking powder
1 teaspoon salt
1 teaspoon sugar
1 teaspoon dried yeast
150 ml/¼ pint milk
150 ml/¼ pint plain yogurt
1 egg, beaten
2 teaspoons poppy seeds (optional)

1. Sift the flour, baking powder, salt and sugar into a bowl. In a cup, mix the yeast to a paste with a little of the milk. Place the yogurt in a saucepan with the remaining milk and heat until lukewarm.
2. Stir in the yeast paste. Add this mixture gradually to the flour and mix to a dough. Knead well, then add the egg and knead again. Cover the dough with a damp cloth and leave in a warm place for 1½ hours or until doubled in size.
3. Break the dough into 6 to 8 pieces, approximately 6 cm/2½ inches in diameter. Roll into balls and flatten with your hand. Dip your fingertips into the poppy seeds (if using) and press into the naan.
4. Place on baking sheets and bake in a preheated oven (230°C/450°F), Gas Mark 8 for 12 minutes or until the naan are puffed and blistered. Keep warm in a low oven. **Makes 6 to 8**

Lemon Syllabub

Metric/Imperial
grated rind and juice of 1 lemon
125 g/4 oz soft brown sugar
150 ml/¼ pint sweet white wine or sherry
300 ml/10 fl oz double cream
sponge fingers, to serve

1. Mix together the lemon rind and juice, sugar and wine or sherry and leave to stand for at least 1 hour. Strain into a mixing bowl, then add the cream.
2. Whisk until the mixture thickens. Spoon into tall glasses and chill well. Serve with sponge fingers. ·14·

Mixed Melon Salad

Metric/Imperial
1 Galia or Ogen melon
1 large wedge watermelon, about 1 kg/2 lb
3 tablespoons Cointreau
fresh mint leaves, to decorate

1. Cut the melon in half, and discard the seeds. Discard the watermelon seeds. Cut both melons into large chunks. Toss together in the Cointreau.
2. Place the melon in individual dishes.
3. Decorate with mint and serve lightly chilled with a little Lemon Syllabub.

C · O · U · N · T · D · O · W · N

A few days before:
Make the Mixed Vegetable Pickle (the process takes 2 days).
The day before:
Make the Dhal. Cool, cover and refrigerate. Cook the Spiced Cauliflower to the end of stage 2. Cool, cover and refrigerate. Cook the brown rice for the Mushroom and Nut Pilaff, cover and keep cool.
On the day:
Mix the lemon rind and juice, sugar and wine for the Lemon Syllabub. Cover and keep cool. Prepare the melon and toss in the Cointreau. Cover the bowls of melon tightly and chill them in the refrigerator. Chill the drinks.
To serve at 8.00 pm:
5.45: Make up the bread dough. Cover with a damp cloth and leave in a warm place until doubled in bulk.
6.30: Decorate the melon salad, cover and chill until required.
7.00: Preheat the oven to (230°C/450°F), Gas Mark 8. Prepare the nuts and vegetables for the Mushroom and Nut Pilaff.
7.10: Cook the remaining ingredients for the Mushroom and Nut Pilaff. Add the rice and simmer gently until heated through. Shape the breads.
7.20: Cook the Naan Breads. Wrap them in foil. Reduce the oven temperature to 150°C/300°F, Gas Mark 2 and return to the oven to keep warm.
7.30: Finish the Lemon Syllabub. Spoon into tall glasses and chill until required. Transfer the Mushroom and Nut Pilaff to a serving dish, cover and keep warm in the oven.
7.40: Reheat the Spiced Cauliflower. Stir in the yogurt. Keep warm in the oven. Reheat the Dhal.
8.00: Garnish the cauliflower with coriander or parsley. Serve the meal.

F · R · E · E · Z · E · R · N · O · T · E · S

Only the Dhal will freeze. Cool, pack and freeze. Thaw overnight at cool room temperature.
Variation:
A simple Onion Chutney could be served with these dishes instead of Mixed Vegetable Pickle: Sprinkle one large peeled and sliced onion with salt. Leave for 30 minutes to soften. Rinse well with cold water and drain. Mix with 2 tablespoons of lime or lemon juice, 2 teaspoons of ground paprika and a little seasoning to taste. Serve in small bowls. (Other spices, such as ground turmeric, cumin, coriander or mild chilli powder may be used instead of paprika.)

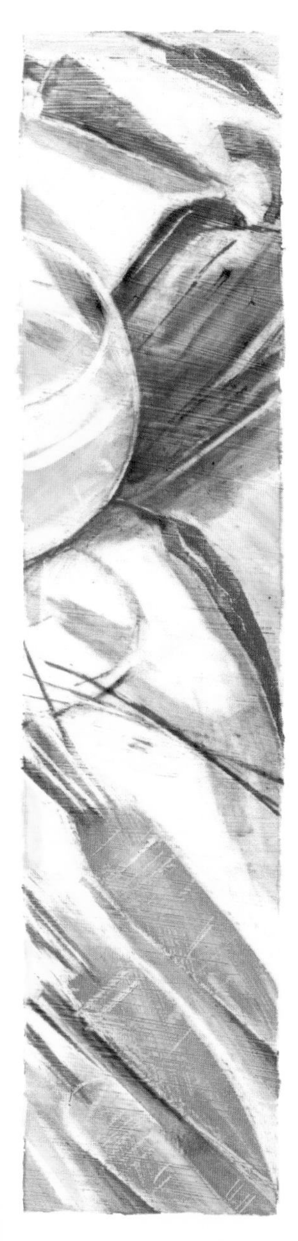

M·E·N·U

· 13 ·

Fireside Supper for 6

Winter Vegetable Casserole
Jacket Potatoes with Garlic
Tossed Green Salad

•

Apple and Coconut Pie
Chantilly Cream

Warm up winter by serving hearty and nourishing stews and hot fruity puddings – perfect fare for welcoming guests in from the cold.

This casual meal is best enjoyed in a relaxed atmosphere around a glowing fire. Set the dishes out on a coffee table (well protected with mats) and invite your guests to help themselves. Mainstay of the meal is a Winter Vegetable Casserole, which provides the perfect opportunity for you to prove what a wide variety of vegetables are available at this time of year.

Pick and Choose

The combination is up to you – the recipe provides a blueprint you can alter to suit your supplies. It is well worth cultivating a small producer of organic vegetables. Not only will the produce be freshly picked, often while you wait, but you will probably be able to obtain some of the more unusual vegetables such as salsify, kohlrabi and scorzonera.

Sweet Surprise

The Apple and Coconut Pie has an unusual, crunchy meringue topping – quite delicious served with featherlight Chantilly Cream.

A warm red wine punch, such as a spicy Glögg or Glühwein would be an excellent warmer to greet your guests.

Winter Vegetable Casserole

Metric/Imperial

2 tablespoons olive oil
3 large onions, quartered
2 cloves garlic, peeled and thinly sliced
1 × 397 g/14 oz can tomatoes
150 ml/¼ pint dry white wine
1 small or ½ large celeriac, peeled and diced
4 celery sticks, trimmed and cut into 5 cm/2 inch lengths
6 carrots, quartered
salt
freshly ground black pepper
1 green pepper, cored, seeded and sliced
2 leeks, trimmed and cut into 5 cm/2 inch lengths
12 whole chestnuts, skinned
few cauliflower florets
1 tablespoon tomato paste
2 teaspoons dried mixed herbs
Topping:
175 g/6 oz plain wholemeal flour
75 g/3 oz butter or margarine
2 tablespoons grated Parmesan cheese
125 g/4 oz mature Cheddar cheese, grated
2 tablespoons chopped fresh parsley

1. Heat the oil in a large pan, add the onion and garlic and fry gently for 5 minutes without browning, taking care not to break up the onions.
2. Stir in the tomatoes with their juice, and wine, then add the celeriac, celery, carrots and salt and pepper to taste. Cover and simmer for 20 minutes.
3. Stir in the green pepper, leeks, chestnuts, cauliflower, tomato paste and herbs and simmer for a further 10 minutes. Transfer to an ovenproof casserole dish.
4. To make the topping, sift the flour and salt into a bowl. Rub in the butter or margarine until the mixture resembles fine breadcrumbs, then stir in the cheeses and parsley. Sprinkle over the vegetable mixture. Bake in a preheated oven (200°C/400°F), Gas Mark 6, for 35 to 40 minutes, until golden brown. Serve hot. ·1·9·

Jacket Potatoes with Garlic

Metric/Imperial

6 large even-sized potatoes, scrubbed
125 g/4 oz butter or margarine
2 cloves garlic, peeled and crushed
1 tablespoon plain flour
300 ml/½ pint milk
salt
freshly ground black pepper
4 tablespoons double cream
4 tablespoons chopped fresh parsley
parsley sprigs, to garnish

1. Prick the potatoes all over with a fork and bake in a preheated oven (200°C/400°F), Gas Mark 6, for 1½ hours or until tender.
2. Melt the butter in a pan, add the crushed garlic, cook gently for 10 minutes without browning. Add the flour and cook for 2 minutes, stirring.
3. Gradually stir in the milk, bring to the boil, then lower the heat and simmer for 2 minutes, stirring constantly. Season well with salt and pepper and stir in the cream. Remove from the heat.
4. Cut the potatoes in half lengthways. Scoop out the flesh and add to the sauce. Work to a purée in an electric blender or food processor. Stir in the parsley.
5. Pile the mixture back into the potato skins. Return to the oven for a further 20 minutes. Serve hot, garnished with parsley sprigs. ·12·

Variation:
If time is limited serve the cooked jacket potatoes with a flavoured butter. Beat one of the following into 75 g/3 oz softened butter: 1 teaspoon mild curry powder, 1 tablespoon chopped fresh coriander or the grated rind of 1 lemon.

Tossed Green Salad

Metric/Imperial
½ lettuce, separated into leaves
¼ bunch of curly endive
½ bunch of watercress
¼ cucumber, sliced
1 green pepper, cored, seeded and sliced
few spring onions
French Dressing:
2 tablespoons wine vinegar
8 tablespoons olive oil
salt
freshly ground black pepper

1. Mix everything together, adding plenty of seasoning. Serve immediately. ·1·2·9·

Cook's Tip:
When making a simple green salad it is easier to make the dressing straight into the salad bowl. If you need dressing for pouring over a salad, or for serving with avocados, for instance, it is easier to make it by shaking all the ingredients together in a clean screw-top jar. Any that's over will keep in the fridge. Some chopped fresh herbs, also a little mustard and a dash of sugar can be added to vary the flavour.

Variation:
A basic green salad can be varied in many ways. Try adding any of the following:
Apple wedges: Use red eating apples, cored and thinly sliced.
Avocado slivers: Halve avocados, remove the stones, peel and slice the flesh. Toss in lemon juice to prevent them turning brown.
Cauliflower sprigs: Break the cauliflower into small sprigs and use raw.
Cheese: Use any kind, grated, sliced or cubed.
Egg: Hard-boil and thinly slice before adding.
Fresh herbs: Wash, dry, chop and add.

Apple and coconut pie

Apple and Coconut Pie

Metric/Imperial
25 g/1 oz butter or margarine
750 g/1½ lb cooking apples, peeled, cored and sliced
2 tablespoons soft brown sugar
1 teaspoon dried mixed spice
125 g/4 oz dates, stoned and roughly chopped
Topping:
1 egg white
50 g/2 oz demerara sugar
50 g/2 oz fresh coconut, finely grated

1. Melt the butter or margarine in a pan and add the apples, sugar and spice. Cover and cook over a very low heat, stirring occasionally, for 10 to 12 minutes. Stir in the dates and place in 900 ml/1½ pint pie dish.
2. Whisk the egg white until stiff, then gradually whisk in the demerara sugar. Fold in the coconut. Spread the coconut meringue over the fruit, using a fork to form a rough surface.
3. Bake in a preheated oven (180°C/350°F), Gas Mark 4, for 20 to 30 minutes until the topping is golden. Serve with Chantilly Cream. ·1·9·

Cook's Tip:
Apple and Coconut Pie is a warming winter pudding with a crunchy coconut topping. Desiccated coconut can be used in place of freshly grated coconut. Try using fresh apricots or peaches to replace the dates.

Chantilly Cream

Metric/Imperial
3 tablespoons water
300 ml/½ pint double cream, chilled
1 tablespoon caster sugar

1. Put the water and beaters from an electric mixer in a bowl and chill in the freezer until ice crystals begin to form. Add the cream and beat until the cream holds soft peaks.
2. Sprinkle on the sugar, and beat it in very lightly.

C · O · U · N · T · D · O · W · N

The day before:
Make the Winter Vegetable Casserole to the end of stage 3. Cool, cover and refrigerate. Prepare the savoury crumble topping and store separately in a covered container in the refrigerator. Make the dressing for the green salad. Cover and store at room temperature. Prepare the Apple and Coconut Pie to the end of stage 1. Cover and keep cool.

On the day:
Make the Glühwein, if serving. Wash and prepare the salad ingredients. Store, separately, in polythene bags in the refrigerator. Prepare the potato filling and return the mixture to the skins. Arrange on a baking sheet, cool, cover and refrigerate.

To serve at 8.00 pm:
7.00: Preheat the oven to (200°C/400°F), Gas Mark 6.
7.20: Sprinkle the topping over the Winter Vegetable Casserole and place in the oven to cook. Make the Chantilly Cream. Cover and refrigerate.
7.40: Place the potatoes in the oven. Prepare the meringue topping and spread over the apple and date mixture. Set aside in a cool place.
7.50: Combine the salad ingredients in a bowl.
8.00: Toss the salad and serve the meal. Reduce the oven temperature to 180°C/350°F, Gas Mark 4 and place the Apple and Coconut Pie in the oven to cook while you enjoy the main dishes.

F · R · E · E · Z · E · R · N · O · T · E · S

Winter Vegetable Casserole: Cool the topped but uncooked casserole, pack in a rigid plastic container and freeze. Thaw overnight in the refrigerator.

Jacket Potatoes with Garlic: Open freeze. When solid, wrap individually in cling film, pack in a rigid container and freeze. To use, reheat from frozen at (200°C/400°F), Gas Mark 6 for 30 minutes.

M·E·N·U

· 14 ·

Hot Fork Buffet for 8

Cheese and Walnut Croquettes
with Watercress Dip
•
Chicory in Mustard Sauce
Wholewheat Salad
Mushrooms with Coriander
Tangy Cucumber Salad
•
St. Clement's Mousse
Red Fruit Compote

When entertaining couples who have never met before, your main concern is not always food, but how well the group will jell. You can select guests with common interests, but until the evening is under way you can never be sure that it will be a success.

Easy Does It

Improve the odds by creating a relaxed atmosphere where guests can move about freely and get to know one another without the constraints of a seating plan. A hot fork buffet is the answer. As an ice-breaker we've chosen a starter that can be handed round as guests arrive. Cheese and Walnut Croquettes are ideal as they can be cooked in advance and warmed through a few at a time. Chicory in Mustard Sauce will present few problems either. Much of the preparation can be done early in the day and the chicory reheated in the sauce and kept warm until required.

Red wines go particularly well with these dishes – serve a dry Italian wine such as a Chianti Classico or offer a Rioja from Spain.

Cheese and Walnut Croquettes with Watercress Dip

Metric/Imperial
250 g/8 oz walnuts, very finely chopped
175 g/6 oz fresh wholemeal breadcrumbs
1 small onion, grated
125 g/4 oz Edam Cheese, finely grated
2 tablespoons chopped fresh parsley
salt
freshly ground black pepper
2 eggs beaten
2 to 3 tablespoons milk
4 tablespoons oil
2 bunches watercress, very finely chopped
300 ml/½ pint soured cream

1. Mix the walnuts with the breadcrumbs, onion, cheese, parsley and salt and pepper to taste. Bind with the eggs and milk. Roll into small balls.
2. Heat the oil in a large frying pan. Add the croquettes and fry for about 10 minutes until browned on all sides. Drain well.
3. Meanwhile for the dip, blend the watercress with the soured cream and salt and pepper to taste. Spoon into a small serving bowl.
4. Serve the croquettes while still warm. ·7·

Chicory in Mustard Sauce

Metric/Imperial
8 heads chicory
juice of 1 lemon
25 g/1 oz butter or margarine
scant 1 tablespoon plain flour
300 ml/½ pint vegetable stock
4 to 6 tablespoons single cream
4 tablespoons made mild mustard
2 tablespoons chopped fresh dill, to garnish

1. Rinse and drain the chicory and remove the thick stems. Bring a pan of salted water to the boil and add the lemon juice. Add the chicory heads, lower the heat and cook for about 10 minutes. Drain, reserving the cooking liquid.
2. Melt the butter or margarine in a small pan, stir in the flour and cook until golden. Gradually add 300 ml/½ pint of the reserved cooking liquid and stock, stirring constantly.
3. Add the cream, mustard and sugar and bring to the boil, stirring constantly. Add the par-cooked chicory and cook for a further 10 minutes over a very low heat until just tender.
4. Transfer to a warmed serving dish and garnish with the chopped dill.

Wholewheat Salad

Metric/Imperial
250 g/8 oz wholewheat, soaked for 1 hour
salt
freshly ground black pepper
6 tablespoons French dressing (see page 55)
4 spring onions, chopped
1 red pepper, cored, seeded and chopped
2 celery sticks, sliced
1 tablespoon chopped fresh parsley
celery tops, to garnish

1. Drain the wholewheat, place in a pan and cover with cold water. Add a little salt and simmer gently for 30 to 40 minutes until softened. Drain well and mix with the dressing while still warm. Leave to cool.
2. Add the remaining ingredients, seasoning with salt and freshly ground black pepper to taste. Mix together thoroughly.
3. Transfer to a salad bowl and garnish with celery tops before serving. ·3·15·

Chicory in mustard sauce

Mushrooms with Coriander

Metric/Imperial

3 tablespoons oil
1 onion, chopped
750 g/1½ lb button mushrooms, quartered
6 tablespoons light stock
1 tablespoon white wine vinegar
1 tablespoon chopped fresh coriander
salt
freshly ground black pepper
chopped fresh parsley, to garnish

1. Heat the oil in a pan, add the onion and cook for about 5 minutes. Add the mushrooms and cook for a further 10 minutes, stirring occasionally.
2. Add the stock and vinegar and bring to the boil, stirring constantly. Add the coriander and seasoning.
3. Cool and serve garnished with the parsley. ·1·4·6· × 2

Tangy Cucumber Salad

Metric/Imperial

12.5 cm/5 inch length of cucumber, diced
½ small red pepper, cored, seeded and sliced
1 small orange, peeled and chopped
1 pink grapefruit, peeled and chopped
3 tablespoons mayonnaise
150 ml/¼ pint natural yogurt
shredded lettuce, to serve

1. Mix the cucumber, red pepper, orange and grapefruit pieces in a salad bowl. Then, cover and refrigerate until required.
2. In a bowl, mix together the mayonnaise and yogurt and stir into the salad. Serve on a bed of shredded lettuce. ·2·5·

St Clements Mousse

Metric/Imperial
finely grated rind and juice of 2 lemons
finely grated rind and juice of 2 oranges
2 teaspoons agar-agar
4 large eggs, separated
125 g/4 oz light soft brown sugar
150 ml/¼ pint plain yogurt

1. Combine the lemon and orange juice in a small pan. Sprinkle the agar-agar over the top and set aside for 5 minutes.
2. Bring the mixture to the boil, stirring constantly. Lower the heat and simmer for 2 minutes.
3. Meanwhile combine the egg yolks, the sugar and citrus rind in the top pan of a double boiler. Set over gently simmering water and whisk until the mixture is thick and pale. Remove from the heat and transfer to a large bowl. Continue whisking until cool.
4. Gradually add the dissolved agar-agar to the egg yolk mixture, whisking constantly. Stir in the yogurt. Leave in a cool place for about 1 hour, until the mixture starts to set.
5. Beat the egg whites until stiff, then fold into the mousse. Pour into a serving bowl and chill in the refrigerator for at least 2 hours before serving. Serve chilled. ·8·10·

Red Fruit Compote

Metric/Imperial
250 g/8 oz sugar
300 ml/½ pint water
500 g/1 lb blackcurrants
grated rind and juice of ½ orange
125 g/4 oz strawberries
125 g/4 oz blackberries
250 g/8 oz raspberries
1 tablespoon arrowroot
2 tablespoons port

1. Place the sugar and water in a pan and heat gently, stirring, until dissolved. Bring to the boil and boil for a few minutes, then add the blackcurrants and orange rind. Simmer gently for 15 minutes until soft.
2. Strain the fruit, reserving the syrup. Place the blackcurrants in a serving dish and add the remaining fruit.
3. Return the syrup to the pan and bring to the boil. Mix the arrowroot with the orange juice and stir into the boiling syrup. Cook, stirring, until thickened and clear. Add the port and pour over the fruit. Allow to cool before serving.

C · O · U · N · T · D · O · W · N

The day before:
Make but do not cook the Cheese and Walnut Croquettes. Prepare the Watercress Dip. Cover both and refrigerate. Make the St. Clement's Mousse and the Red Fruit Compote. Cover and refrigerate.
On the day:
Cook the croquettes. Cover and keep cool. Make the Mushrooms with Coriander. Cover and refrigerate. Complete the remaining two salads. Refrigerate.
To serve at 8.00 pm:
6.00: Cook the chicory. Make the sauce. Off the heat, stir the chicory into the sauce, cover and keep cool. Decorate the St. Clement's Mousse and return to the refrigerator. Open the red wines.
7.30: Preheat the oven to (180°C/350°F), Gas Mark 4.
7.45: Reheat a few croquettes. Gently bring the Chicory in Mustard Sauce to the boil. Transfer to an ovenproof serving dish. Cover and keep warm.
7.50: Set out the wines and salads.
8.00: Serve the meal.

F · R · E · E · Z · E · R · N · O · T · E · S

Cheese and Walnut Croquettes: Open freeze in a single layer on a baking sheet. Pack. Thaw overnight in the refrigerator.

M·E·N·U

· 15 ·

Pancake Lunch for 4

Hungarian Spinach Pancakes
Honey-lemon Slaw
Bean Shoot and Mushroom Salad

If you can toss a pancake you can throw a party. The superb dish that is the backbone of this simple buffet looks spectacular, yet owes its success to the common pancake. It is a layered pancake pie, topped with grated cheese, baked in the oven and served in slices, like a cake with a mustard sauce. This menu could easily be extended to serve larger numbers. For a special event such as a Christening or a celebration lunch; add Peanut Roast (page 26), Tomatoes with Basil (page 43) and Lettuce and Orange Salad (page 23).

Well Prepared

All the party food is prepared in advance, and the principal dish can be frozen months ahead, making this the ideal menu for novice cooks or hostesses with less time than they would like. Even the salads can be prepared in advance, and stored in the refrigerator until required.

Punch Lines

A light white wine punch would get the occasion off to a sparkling start. Simply steep 3 tablespoons of tea leaves in 1.2 litres/2 pints boiling water for 5 minutes. Add 2 bottles Sauternes and 120 ml/4 fl oz fresh lime juice. Fifteen minutes before serving, strain over ice cubes in a large punch bowl and float slices of fresh lime on the surface. Alternatively, serve with sparkling white wine.

Hungarian Spinach Pancakes

Metric/Imperial

300 ml/½ pint milk and water, mixed
1 egg
125 g/4 oz plain wholemeal flour
salt
1 tablespoon oil
1 lb fresh spinach
1 tablespoon oil
1 onion, chopped
1 teaspoon paprika pepper
125 g/4 oz Ricotta cheese, or
125 g/4 oz Cottage cheese
freshly ground black pepper
600 ml/1 pint Mustard Sauce (page 58), to serve, or
600 ml/1 pint Fresh Tomato Sauce (page 35)

1. Place the milk and water, egg, flour, salt and oil in an electric blender and blend for 2 minutes until completely smooth.
2. Cook the spinach in a covered saucepan. Drain and chop finely. Heat the oil in a pan and fry the onion with the paprika until soft. Cool. Stir in the Ricotta cheese and spinach, season well and mix.
3. Using the prepared batter, fry 6 pancakes. Place one on a heatproof plate, spread with some of the filling and cover with another pancake. Continue layering in this way, finishing with a pancake. Sprinkle with the cheese and bake in a preheated oven (190°C/375°F), Gas Mark 5 for 20 minutes. Serve with the Mustard or Fresh Tomato Sauce.

Variation:
Add a little cooked spinach to the batter and roll the filling in the pancakes.

Hungarian spinach pancakes

Honey-lemon Slaw

Metric/Imperial
2 tablespoons mayonnaise
1 tablespoon honey
½ teaspoon grated lemon rind
1 tablespoon lemon juice
¼ teaspoon ground ginger
175 g/6 oz red cabbage, shredded
175 g/6 oz white cabbage, shredded
salt
freshly ground black pepper

1. In a large bowl, mix the mayonnaise, honey, lemon rind and juice, and ginger. Stir in the red and white cabbage and mix until evenly coated.
2. Sprinkle with salt and pepper to taste and serve chilled. ·1·3·

Bean Shoot and Mushroom Salad

Metric/Imperial
250 g/8 oz bean shoots, washed and drained
350 g/12 oz button mushrooms, quartered
1 red pepper, cored, seeded and diced
chopped fresh parsley, to garnish
Dressing:
4 tablespoons olive oil
1 tablespoon cider vinegar
1 clove garlic, crushed
1 teaspoon soy sauce
salt
freshly ground black pepper

1. Place the vegetables in a salad bowl.
2. To make the dressing, mix the oil, vinegar, garlic, soy sauce and seasoning in a screw-top jar and shake well. Pour over the salad ingredients and toss until well coated. Serve sprinkled with the parsley.

C · O · U · N · T · D · O · W · N

The day before:
Make the pancakes and filling for the Hungarian Spinach Pancakes. Layer the pancakes between sheets of greaseproof paper and store in a cool place. Cool, cover and store the filling in the refrigerator. Mix the mayonnaise dressing for the Honey-Lemon Slaw. Cover and keep cool. Make the dressing for the Bean Shoot and Mushroom Salad. Store at cool room temperature.
On the day:
Prepare the vegetables for the Bean Shoot and Mushroom Salad and store in polythene bags in the refrigerator.
To serve at 1 pm:
11.00: Shred the cabbage for the Honey-Lemon Slaw. Toss in the mayonnaise. Cover and keep in the refrigerator. Assemble the layered spinach pancakes. Cover and keep in a cool place. Chill the wines.
12.25: Preheat the oven to (190°C/375°F), Gas Mark 5.
12.40: Place the pancakes in the oven to heat. Toss the Bean Shoot and Mushroom Salad.
12.50: Set out the salads and open wines.
1.00: Serve the meal.

F · R · E · E · Z · E · R · N · O · T · E · S

Hungarian Spinach Pancakes: Assemble the pancakes and filling but do not add the cheese. Open freeze, then wrap. Thaw overnight at cool room temperature and sprinkle with cheese before cooking in a pre-heated oven (190°C/375°F) Gas Mark 5 for 20 minutes.
Cook's Tip:
Pancakes are well worth storing in the freezer and are ideal for turning leftovers into stunning suppers. Make double the quantity of pancakes required here and freeze the extras between sheets of greaseproof paper. They will thaw in minutes, and can be filled with leftover vegetables. Place in an ovenproof dish, coat with a thin cheese or parsley sauce and reheat before serving.

I · N · D · E · X

A·C·K·N·O·W·L·E·D·G·E·M·E·N·T·S

Robert Golden 18, 58, 62; Melvin Grey 42, 48; Paul Williams 6, 10, 15, 23, 26, 31, 34, 44, 51, 55.

Jacket photography: Clive Streeter   Illustration: Jane Human
General Editor: Jenni Fleetwood   Art Editor: David Rowley   Production Controller: Sara Hunt